Lonely planet

POCKET

KYOTO & OSAKA

TOP SIGHTS · LOCAL EXPERIENCES

D0370460

KATE MORGAN

Contents

Plan Your Trip   4

Kimono fabric
OKUI/SHUTTERSTOCK ©

Welcome to Kyoto & Osaka

Kyoto is old Japan writ large: quiet temples, sublime gardens, colourful shrines, postcard-perfect street scenes and geisha scurrying to secret liaisons. While Osaka's grey concrete jungle is no match in terms of beauty, this fast-paced, brash city, cloaked in dazzling neon, packs a punch with its excellent food and nightlife scenes, and locals full of personality.

Yasaka-jinja from Sannen-zaka (p79)

Top Sights

Kinkaku-ji, Kyoto

Golden brilliance and stunning gardens. **p106**

Fushimi Inari-Taisha, Kyoto

A sprawling Shintō shrine spectacle. **p36**

Ginkaku-ji, Kyoto

A temple garden paradise. **p90**

Gion, Kyoto

Glimpse the world of geisha. **p72**

Chion-in, Kyoto

Pilgrimage temple buzzing with activity. **p70**

PHIL WEYMOUTH/LONELY PLANET ©

Kiyomizu-dera, Kyoto

Ancient temple overlooking the city. **p68**

GAGLIARDIIMAGES/SHUTTERSTOCK ©

Dōtombori, Osaka

Famous neon-lit night scene. **p126**

Nanzen-ji, Kyoto

Zen temple complex with views. **p92**

Nishiki Market, Kyoto

Wonderful ingredients of Kyoto cuisine. **p48**

Nijō-jō, Kyoto

Japan's feudal military might. **p50**

COWARDLION/SHUTTERSTOCK ©

Daitoku-ji, Kyoto

Exploring a world of Zen gardens. **p110**

Osaka-jō, Osaka

Historic castle and Osaka landmark. **p140**

COWARDLION/SHUTTERSTOCK ©

Eating

Kyoto is one of the world's great food cities. In fact, when you consider atmosphere, service and quality, it's hard to think of a city where you get more bang for your dining buck. You can pretty much find a great dining option in any neighbourhood, but the majority of the best spots are clustered downtown. Osaka has a rich food culture, too, which ranks as the number one reason to visit.

LOTTIE DAVIES/LONELY PLANET ©

Kaiseki (Kyoto)

Where ingredients, setting and presentation come together to create a refined dining experience unlike any other. *Kaiseki* (Japanese haute cuisine) is usually eaten in the private room of a *ryōtei* (traditional, high-class restaurant) or ryokan.

Tofu-ryōri (Kyoto)

Kyoto is famed for its tofu (soybean curd), a result of the city's excellent water and large population of (theoretically) vegetarian Buddhist monks.

There are many exquisite *yudōfu* (tofu cooked in a pot) restaurants in Northern Higashiyama along the roads around Nanzenji, and in the Arashiyama area.

Tako-yaki (Osaka)

Doughy dumplings (pictured right) stuffed with octopus (*tako* in Japanese) often sold as street food, topped with savoury sauce, powdered *aonori* (seaweed), mayonnaise and bonito flakes, and eaten with toothpicks. The centre can be molten hot.

Okonomiyaki (Osaka)

Thick, savoury pancakes filled with shredded cabbage and your choice of meat, seafood or vegetables. Often prepared on a *teppan* (steel plate) set into your table.

Best Kaiseki

Kitcho Arashiyama, Kyoto No-holds-barred *kaiseki* served in superb private rooms. (p123)

Kikunoi, Kyoto Wonderful *kaiseki* in a classic setting. (pictured above; p81)

Shoubentango-tei, Osaka Osaka-style *kaiseki* in a 100-year-old restaurant. (p133)

VICHAILAO/SHUTTERSTOCK ©

Giro Giro Hitoshina, **Kyoto** Affordable *kaiseki*, minus the pomp and formality. (p58)

Best Sushi

Sushi no Musashi, **Kyoto** Convenient and cheap downtown sushi-train restaurant. (p59)

Tsukiji Sushisei, **Kyoto** High-quality sushi in an approachable setting. (p59)

Daiki Suisan, **Osaka** Large sushi-train restaurant with a prime location. (p134)

Best Soba & Udon

Honke Owariya, **Kyoto** Filling soba and udon in a quiet downtown spot. (p57)

Omen Kodai-ji, **Kyoto** Wonderful noodles in a

smart setting in Southern Higashiyama. (p81)

Imai Honten, **Osaka** One of the oldest udon noodle specialists. (p133)

Best Ramen

Ippūdō, **Kyoto** Tasty Kyūshū-style ramen and crispy *gyōza* (dumplings). (p60)

Kyoto Rāmen Kōji, **Kyoto** Choice of nine ramen joints in Kyoto Station. (p42)

Kinryū Ramen, **Osaka** People-watch in Dōtombori as you slurp back cheap noodles. (p133)

Best Okonomiyaki

Chibō, **Osaka** City's most famous *okonomiyaki* spot, with long queues. (p132)

Nishiki Warai, **Kyoto** Convenient casual eatery near Nishiki Market. (p59)

Top Tips

○ Check out department store basements for gourmet shops, while the upper floors usually have a *resutorangai* (restaurant city).

○ Many of Kyoto's *kaiseki* restaurants serve a delicious lunch set that costs a fraction of the dinner price.

Drinking & Nightlife

Kyoto and Osaka are both cities with endless options for drinking, whether it's an expertly crafted single-origin coffee in a cafe, matcha (powdered green tea) at a traditional tearoom, carefully crafted cocktails and single malts in a sophisticated six-seater bar, or Japanese craft beer in a brewery.

Beer

Beer is the overwhelming favourite drink to have with dinner, but gone are the days of simply having the well-known brands, Asahi, Sapporo, Kirin etc, on the menu. Craft beer is changing the beer landscape in Kyoto and Osaka, with breweries and bars specialising in Japanese craft beer.

Sake

While beer is the popular choice, sake (*nihonshū*; pictured) is making a comeback in the old capital. It's especially popular with sushi and *kaiseki* and at *izakaya* (Japanese pubeateries). Sake is usually consumed cold in Japan, especially the good stuff, but some people order it hot (the Japanese word for this is *atsukan*) at more casual places like *izakaya* and *yakitori* restaurants.

Shōchū

Shōchū is popular throughout Japan and is a clear spirit typically made from potato and barley. At around an average alcohol content of 30%, it's a drink that packs a potent punch. It's usually served diluted with hot water (*oyuwari*) or in a *chūhai* cocktail mixed with soft drinks. It's on the menu at *izakaya* and you can buy *chūhai* cans in supermarkets and *konbini* (convenience stores).

Best Cocktail Bars

Bar K6, **Kyoto** Single malts and expertly mixed cocktails are the draw at this smart local gathering spot. (p62)

Tōzan Bar, **Kyoto** The basement bar at the Hyatt Regency Kyoto is worth a trip for the design alone. (p84)

SHAIITH/SHUTTERSTOCK ©

Bee's Knees, Kyoto
Speakeasy-style bar with creative cocktails. (p61)

40 Sky Bar & Lounge, Osaka Classy bar with stunning views at the Conrad Osaka hotel. (p149)

Best Craft Beer

Bungalow, Kyoto Cool industrial downtown bar with great beer. (p60)

Kyoto Brewing Company, Kyoto Great little tasting room with a local vibe. (p43)

Beer Belly, Osaka Osaka's best microbrewery. (p149)

Craft Beer Base, Osaka
Bottle shop/bar with a great range of craft beer. (p151)

Best Clubs

World, Kyoto Huge club with a calendar of events. (p62)

Circus, Osaka In the centre of the city's underground electronica scene. (p135)

Best Tea & Coffee

Weekenders Coffee, Kyoto Some of the city's best coffee in a tiny downtown spot. (p61)

Brooklyn Roasting Company, Osaka Hip riverside cafe with an industrial feel. (p149)

Kiln, Kyoto Great brews to go with pretty canal views. (p61)

Kaboku Tearoom, Kyoto Cafe attached to Kyoto's famous Ippōdō Tea store. (p53)

Kurasu, Kyoto Expertly made coffee close to Kyoto Station. (p43)

Kissa Madura, Osaka Long-running retro cafe popular with locals. (p149)

Kyoto in a Glass
Matcha

Usually *Matcha* is served as *usucha* ('thin' tea), which is already much thicker than an infusion.

At formal tea ceremonies (and at some tea shops) *matcha* is also served as *koicha* ('thick' tea), which is as thick as cream.

Matcha in Kyoto

Kyoto is traditionally known for its high-quality green tea and the art of the ancient tea ceremony. *Matcha* is high in caffeine and is served at tea ceremonies and in teahouses at many temples in the city. The powdered tea is whisked into an emulsion and drunk unstrained.

If you prefer milk with your *matcha*, many cafes serve the bright-green tea in latte form.

Whisking powdered *matcha*

GREG ELMS/LONELY PLANET ©

Shopping & Markets

Kyoto and Osaka have a fantastic variety of both traditional and modern shops, and some fantastic markets. Whether you're looking for fans, kimonos and tea, or the latest electronics, hip fashion and ingenious gadgets, these two cities have plenty to offer.

SANN VON MAI/SHUTTERSTOCK ©

Where to Shop in Kyoto

Shopping neighbourhoods in Kyoto tend to be organised by speciality, which makes things easier if you're after specific items. Here are some of Kyoto's most important shopping streets and what you'll find there:

Teramachi-dōri, north of Oike-dōri
Traditional Japanese crafts, tea-ceremony goods, green tea and antiques.

Teramachi-dōri, south of Shijō-dōri
Electronics and computers.

Shijō-dōri, between Kawaramachi-dōri and Karasuma-dōri
Department stores, fashion boutiques and traditional arts and crafts.

Shinmonzen-dōri
Antiques.

Gojō-zaka
Pottery.

Where to Shop in Osaka

Osaka Station
The station is ringed by malls and department stores (all interconnected by underground passages), making the Umeda district one big shopping conurbation. You'll find outlets of the most popular national chains here, including Uniqlo, Muji, Tokyu Hands and Yodobashi Umeda, along with literally hundreds of fashion boutiques.

Midō-suji
International high-end brands line the main boulevard between Shinsaibashi and Namba Stations.

Shinsaibashi-suji
This jam-packed arcade has popular local and international chain stores.

GREG ELMS/LONELY PLANET ©

GREG ELMS/LONELY PLANET ©

Ame-Mura & Minami-Horie

On the west side of Midō-suji there's youthful streetwear and secondhand shops, while Minami-Horie has trendy boutiques.

Namba Station

Anchored by the huge mall Namba Parks.

Den Den Town

(でんでんタウン) Osaka's electronics district.

Best Department Stores

Daimaru, Kyoto A sumptuous selection at this vast downtown store. (p65)

Takashimaya, Kyoto An elegant and rich assortment of shops, along with great restaurants and a food floor to boggle the mind. (p63)

Hankyū Umeda, Osaka Food, fashion and homewares in one of Japan's largest department stores. (p153)

Tokyu Hands, Osaka Gadgets, lifestyle products and homewares. (p138)

Best Traditional Arts & Crafts

Wagami no Mise, Kyoto A beautiful selection of *washi* (Japanese handmade paper) at this downtown shop. (p64)

Zōhiko, Kyoto A wonderland for the lover of lacquerware. (p63)

Takashimaya, Kyoto The 6th floor of this department store has great lacquerware, pottery, wood crafts and so on. (p63)

Best Markets

Kōbō-san, Kyoto From used kimonos to ceramics and antiques, this market has it all. (pictured left; p45)

Nishiki Market, Kyoto Food is only the start of the offerings at Kyoto's most famous market. (p48)

Dōguya-suji Arcade, Osaka Market stalls crammed with cookware and kitchen goods. (p138)

Top Kyoto Souvenirs

Kimonos

Choose from racks of vintage styles at flea markets or high-end silk beauties at a boutique.

Washi

Washi is a lightweight, affordable souvenir.

Lacquerware

Stunning lacquerware bowls, cups and boxes make beautiful gifts. Zōhiko (p63) downtown has an incredible selection.

Tea

Matcha is the perfect Kyoto souvenir and Ippōdō Tea (p64) in the downtown area is *the* place to buy it.

Japanese Knives

Pick up one of Japan's most renowned brands of chef's knives at Aritsugu (p63) in Nishiki Market.

Architecture & Gardens

You will find countless pockets of astonishing beauty in Kyoto: ancient temples with graceful wooden halls, traditional town houses clustered together along narrow streets, colourful Shintō shrines and, best of all, a profusion of gardens. Osaka may not have the beauty of Kyoto, but it has some striking architecture.

RICARDO PERNA/SHUTTERSTOCK ©

Machiya

Machiya are wooden terrace houses that functioned as both homes and workplaces for Japan's bourgeoisie, a class that grew in prominence during the Edo period. The shop area was located in the front of the house, while the rooms lined up behind it formed the family's private living quarters. Although well suited to Kyoto's humid, mildew-prone summers, a wooden *machiya* has a limited lifespan of about 50 years. In the decades after WWII, many

families chose not to rebuild them and instead put up multistorey concrete buildings. The pendulum swung back around in the 1990s, when it became clear that the city was losing something dear. Since then there have been numerous efforts to restore old *machiya*; many of them now house restaurants, cafes and boutiques.

Japanese Gardens

You'll encounter a few major types of garden during your horticultural explorations.

Shūyū

These 'stroll' gardens are intended to be viewed from a winding path, allowing the design to unfold and reveal itself from different vantages.

Kanshō

Zen rock gardens (also known as *kare-sansui* gardens) are an example of a type of 'contemplative' garden intended to be viewed from one vantage point and designed to aid meditation.

Kaiyū

The 'varied pleasures' garden has many small gardens with

GREG ELMS/LONELY PLANET ©

one or more tea-houses surrounding a central pond.

Best Traditional Architecture

Ōkōchi Sansō, **Kyoto** Lavish estate with stunning house and teahouse. (pictured left; p123)

Gion, **Kyoto** Traditional houses line this atmospheric old quarter. (pictured right; p72)

Nishijin, **Kyoto** The city's traditional textile neighbourhood, with traditional houses. (p117)

Best Modern Architecture

Umeda Sky Building, **Osaka** Landmark building

resembling a futuristic Arc de Triomphe. (p145)

Kyoto Station An awe-inspiring steel-and-glass cathedral-like space. (p40)

Best Gardens

Tōfuku-ji, **Kyoto** Temple complex with spectacular garden. (p40)

Ginkaku-ji, **Kyoto** Features sensational raked cones of white sand. (p90)

Ōkōchi Sansō, Kyoto Sprawling gardens with mountain views. (p123)

Shōren-in, **Kyoto** Giant camphor trees and a stunning landscape garden await at this quiet temple. (p77)

Shakkei: Borrowed Scenery

Flowering plants are only one component of the Japanese garden, which may be composed of any combination of vegetation (including trees, shrubs and moss), stones of varying sizes and water. Some gardens are not limited to that which falls within their walls, but take into account the scenery beyond, a technique called *shakkei* (borrowed scenery).

Arts & Culture

Kyoto is Japan's heart and soul, a great centre for the arts for over a millennium. Japan has at times looked outward and at times looked inward, drawing inspiration from the world and then refining it to the nth degree. The result is a rich, sophisticated artistic tradition that transcends museum walls and seeps into daily life.

GREG ELMS/LONELY PLANET ©

Textiles

Kyoto is famous for its *kyō-yūzen* textiles. *Yūzen* is a method of silk-dyeing *(sen-shoku)* developed to perfection in the 17th century by fan painter Miyazaki Yūzen.

Nishijin weaving *(Nishijin-ori)* is internationally renowned and dates to the founding of the city. Nishijin techniques were originally developed to satisfy the demands of the nobility, who favoured the quality of illustrious silk fabrics.

Pottery & Ceramics

In the mid-1600s, there were more than 10 different kilns active in and around Kyoto. Of these, however, only Kiyomizu-yaki remains today. This kiln first gained prominence through the potter Nonomura Ninsei (1596–1660), who developed an innovative method of applying enamel overglaze to porcelain. This technique was further embellished by adding decorative features such as transparent glaze *(sometsuke)*, as well as incorporating designs in red paint *(aka-e)* and celadon *(seiji)*.

Best Artistic & Cultural Experiences in Kyoto

Nishijin Kyoto's traditional textile-weaving district, filled with traditional town houses. (p117)

Camellia Tea Experience Learn the art of the tea ceremony. (p83)

Fureai-Kan Kyoto Museum of Traditional Crafts Check out displays on traditional arts and crafts. (p99)

Funaoka Onsen Enjoy the relaxing cultural experience of an onsen. (p119)

Temples & Shrines

LUCIANO MORTULA – LGM/SHUTTERSTOCK ©

Kyoto's temples and shrines are the main draw for many visitors to the city, and for good reason: they are among the best examples of religious architecture on earth. With over 1000 Buddhist temples and more than 400 Shintō shrines, exploring these wonders is the work of a lifetime. Osaka also has a couple of shrines and temples worth visiting.

Best Temples, Kyoto

Nanzen-ji A pleasant temple complex with expansive grounds. (p92)

Kinkaku-ji The 'Golden Pavilion's' reflection shimmers in its own pond. (p106)

Ginkaku-ji The 'Silver Pavilion' has stunning Zen gardens. (pictured; p90)

Chion-in A massive complex with impressive halls and artworks. (p70)

Shōren-in A place to escape the crowds and meditate overlooking the stunning garden. (p77)

Eikan-dō Superb temple with city views from its pagoda. (p98)

Daitoku-ji A collection of Zen temples and perfect gardens. (p110)

Kiyomizu-dera One of the city's most popular temples. (p68)

Best Shrines, Kyoto

Fushimi Inari-Taisha Hundreds of *torii* (entrance gates spread over a mountainside. (p36)

Kamigamo-jinja A shrine that predates the founding of Kyoto. (p117)

Yasaka-jinja Shintō shrine in Gion. (p79)

Best Temples & Shrines, Osaka

Hōzen-ji An urban temple covered in moss. (p129)

O-hatsu Ten-jin A 1300-year-old shrine hidden among skyscrapers. (p145)

For Kids

GORAN BOGICEVIC/SHUTTERSTOCK ©

Kyoto and Osaka are great for kids and the usual worries aren't an issue in ultrasafe and spotless Japan. Your biggest challenge will be keeping your children entertained. The very things that many adults come to Kyoto to see (temples, gardens and shrines) can be a bit boring for kids, but there are other attractions they will enjoy.

How to Keep the Kids Happy

There is no short-age of child friendly attractions in Kyoto and Osaka, from game centres to parks and a steam locomotive museum. If your kids are older, you have lots of options: go on a hike in the mountains around Kyoto, or rent a bicycle to explore the cities.

Fushimi Inari-Taisha, Kyoto
Kids will be entranced by the hypnotic arcades of *torii* at this sprawling Shintō shrine. (p36)

Kiyomizu-dera, Kyoto With fortunes to take, holy water to drink and an incredible underground sanctuary, this hands-on temple will keep even the most hyper kids happy for an hour or two. (p68)

Kyoto Railway Museum
With vintage steam loco-motives, this museum is a must for train-crazy kids. (pictured: p41)

Kyoto Botanical Gardens
For a picnic, a stroll or a Fris-bee toss, these gardens are just the ticket. (p117)

Amerika-Mura, Osaka
Older kids will love scouring the youth-focused shops here. (p131)

Worth a Trip: Kaiyūkan

Osaka Aquarium Kaiyūkan (海遊館; www.kaiyukan.com; 1-1-10 Kaigan-dōri, Minato-ku; ⏰10am-8pm, last entry 7pm; adult ¥2300, child ¥600-1200; 🚈Chūō line to Osaka-kō, exit 1) features an 800m-plus walkway which winds past displays of sea life from around the Pacific 'ring of fire'. Most impressive is the ginormous central tank, housing a whale shark, manta and thousands of other fish. Note there are also captive dolphins here; there is growing evidence that keeping ceta-ceans in captivity is harmful for the animals.

For Free

ABDERAZAK TISSOUKAI/500PX ©

You may think that the cost of sight-seeing in Kyoto and Osaka is going to require taking a second mortgage on your home. Luckily there's plenty you can do for free – you could fill at least a week with activities that won't cost a penny. Here are just a few...

Best Temples

Nanzen-ji, Kyoto The sprawling grounds of this superb Northern Higashi-yama temple make it a favourite for a stroll. (p92)

Chion-in, Kyoto You can tour the grounds at this immense temple complex for free. (p70)

Tōfuku-ji, Kyoto At the south end of the Higashi-yama Mountains, this fine Zen temple has expansive grounds. (p40)

Best Shrines

Fushimi Inari-Taisha, Kyoto The only money you're likely to drop here is to buy a drink after climbing the mountain. (p36)

Shimogamo-jinja, Kyoto Take a stroll through the magnificent Tadasu-no-mori (Forest of Truth), which leads to the main hall. (p116)

Yasaka-jinja, Kyoto This popular shrine is highly recommended in the evening, when the lanterns make it magical. (p79)

Best Parks

Kyoto Imperial Palace Park, Kyoto A treasure that many visitors to the city overlook. It has everything from baseball diamonds to carp ponds. (p116)

Maruyama-kōen, Kyoto Smack on the main sight-seeing route, this lovely park is a great spot for a picnic. (p78)

Triangle Park, Osaka Concrete 'park' in Ame-Mura, perfect for people-watching. (p131)

Osaka-jō, Osaka While the castle itself might cost you, the vast surrounding park is free to wander and picnic in. (p140)

Best Other Attractions

Nishiki Market, Kyoto It costs nothing to wander through this wonderful market. (p48)

Arashiyama Bamboo Grove, Kyoto Take a magical stroll around one of the most popular sights in Kyoto. (pictured; p123)

Dōtombori, Osaka Stroll this neon-lit canal-side evening spot. (p126)

Four Perfect Days

Day 1, Kyoto

Start your Kyoto experience by heading to Southern Higashiyama (p67). Kick off with temples **Chion-in** (p70) and **Shōren-in** (p77) before a wander through **Maruyama-kōen** (p78), then lunch at **Hisago** (p82).

Stroll through the lanes of **Ninen-zaka** and **Sannen-zaka** (pictured; p79), stopping in at teahouses and boutiques. Spend the afternoon exploring one of the city's premier sights, **Kiyomizu-dera** (p68), before getting your first taste of an *izakaya* (pub-eatery) at **Gion Yuki** (p82) for dinner.

After dinner take in the atmospheric **Gion** (p72) district and keep an eye out for geisha shuffling around the traditional lantern-lit streets. Round off the evening with a drink at the **Gion Finlandia Bar** (p84).

Day 2, Kyoto

There are several great temples to see in Northern Higashiyama (p89). Beat the crowds with an early visit to **Ginkaku-ji** (p90) before making your way along the **Path of Philosophy** (pictured; p98) and then exploring the vast **Nanzen-ji** (p92) temple complex and gardens. Fuel up on noodles for lunch at **Hinode Udon** (p103).

Take a break from temples and head downtown to check out the famous **Nishiki Market** (p48). Carry on shopping along the covered arcade and the department stores on Kawaramachi-dōri and Shijō-dōri.

Book ahead for a *kaiseki* (haute cuisine) dinner with a twist at **Giro Giro Hitoshina** (p58), before an after-dinner stroll along atmospheric **Ponto-chō** (p56).

Day 3, Kyoto

The immediate Kyoto Station area doesn't offer much in the way of sightseeing, but head further south and you'll find two stunning attractions: **Tōfuku-ji** (p40) and **Fushimi Inari-Taisha** (pictured; p36). Afterwards make your way back to the station to take your pick of ramen restaurants for lunch at **Kyoto Rāmen Kōji** (p42).

From Kyoto Station, take the subway or board a bus for **Daitoku-ji** (p110), a maze of lanes with temples featuring incredible Zen gardens. Wander around before jumping back on the subway to head downtown for a spot of dinner. Book in advance for delicate tempura at **Yoshikawa** (p58).

After dinner head over to **Sake Bar Yoramu** (p62), or drop into **Bee's Knees** (p61) bar for excellent cocktails.

Day 4, Osaka

Spend day four on a visit to Osaka. Start by exploring the **Osaka-jō** (p140). Take the subway or enjoy a stroll along the river to Naka-no-shima for coffee with river views at **Brooklyn Roasting Company** (p149). Book in advance for a delicious tempura lunch at **Yotaro Honten** (p146) nearby.

After lunch take the subway down to Shinsaibashi to stroll through **Shinsaibashi-suji Shōtengai** (p138) and over **Ebisu-bashi** (p127) before joining the nightly throngs in neon-lit **Dōtombori** (p126).

There are plenty of places to eat here, like for *kaiseki* at **Shoubentango-tei** (p133) or **Chibō** (p132) for *okonomiyaki* (pictued; savoury pancakes). See where the night takes you in bar- and club-packed **Amerika-Mura** (p131).

Need to Know

For detailed information, see Survival Guide p157

Currency
Yen (¥)

Language
Japanese

Visas
Issued on arrival for most nationalities for stays of up to 90 days.

Money
ATMs available in major banks, post offices and 7-Eleven stores. Credit cards usually accepted, except in some eateries.

Mobile Phones
Can be rented online or at the airport for making voice calls. Prepaid data-only SIM cards can be purchased and used with unlocked smartphones.

Time
Japan Standard Time (GMT/UTC plus nine hours)

Tipping
Uncommon and never expected. At high-end restaurants and hotels a 10% service charge is usually added to the bill.

Daily Budget

Budget: Less than ¥10,000
Dorm bed: ¥3000
Two simple restaurant meals: ¥2200
Train/bus transport: ¥1200
One temple/museum admission: ¥500
Snacks, drinks, sundries: ¥1000

Midrange: ¥10,000–25,000
Double room in a midrange hotel: ¥12,000
Two midrange restaurant meals: ¥5000
Train/bus transport: ¥1200
Two temple/museum admissions: ¥1000
Snacks, drinks, sundries: ¥2000

Top End: More than ¥25,000
Five-star hotel/ryokan accommodation: ¥30,000
Kaiseki restaurant meal: ¥10,000
Train/bus transport: ¥1200
Two taxi rides: ¥3500
Two temple/museum admissions: ¥1000

Advance Planning

Several months before Make accommodation reservations, particularly if you are travelling in cherry-blossom season (March and April) or the autumn-foliage season (October and November).

One month before Book at popular restaurants to avoid missing out, particularly high-end *kaiseki* (haute cuisine) restaurants and Michelin-starred places.

A few days before Book a cooking course or tea ceremony.

Arriving in Kyoto & Osaka

Kansai International Airport The main entry point serving both cities. It's about 75 minutes away from Kyoto by direct express train. From Osaka, it's around 50 minutes.

Itami Airport Also confusingly called Osaka International Airport, this domestic airport is about 12km northwest of Osaka.

Kyoto Station Linked to nearby cities by several train lines, including Japan Railways.

Shin-Osaka Station On the Tōkaidō-Sanyō *shinkansen* line (between Tokyo and Hakata in Fukuoka), and the eastern terminus of the Kyūshū *shinkansen* to Kagoshima. Departures are frequent.

Getting Around

At only 40 kilometres or so apart, it's easy to travel from Kyoto to Osaka (and vice-versa).

Kyoto train station is served by the Tōkaidō and San-yō *shinkansen* (bullet train) lines, which connect the city to Osaka (Shin-Osaka Station; ¥1420, 14 minutes).

From Osaka, the JR Kyoto line is cheaper and easier than getting the *shinkansen*. To Kyoto, it takes around 30 minutes (¥560).

Kyoto

Subway Operates from 5.30am to 11.30pm. Minimum adult fare is ¥210 (children ¥110).

Bus Useful for destinations not well served by the subway lines. Most buses run between 7am and 10pm. Inner-city buses charge a flat fare (¥230 for adults, ¥120 for children ages six to 12, free for those younger).

Bicycle A brilliant way to explore the city (which is mostly flat).

Taxi For short trips, late at night, or if you've got heavy luggage, a taxi is your best bet.

Osaka

Train The JR Kanjō-sen – the Osaka loop line – makes a circuit south of JR Osaka Station, though most sights fall in the middle of it.

Subway There are eight subway lines in Osaka. Single rides cost ¥180 to ¥370 (half-price for children).

Taxi The only option after midnight when public transport shuts down. Flagfall is ¥680, which covers the first 2km; then it's ¥80 for every additional 296m.

Kyoto Neighbourhoods

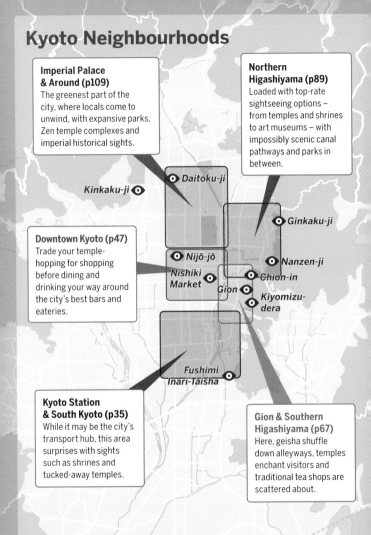

Imperial Palace & Around (p109)
The greenest part of the city, where locals come to unwind, with expansive parks, Zen temple complexes and imperial historical sights.

Northern Higashiyama (p89)
Loaded with top-rate sightseeing options – from temples and shrines to art museums – with impossibly scenic canal pathways and parks in between.

Downtown Kyoto (p47)
Trade your temple-hopping for shopping before dining and drinking your way around the city's best bars and eateries.

Kyoto Station & South Kyoto (p35)
While it may be the city's transport hub, this area surprises with sights such as shrines and tucked-away temples.

Gion & Southern Higashiyama (p67)
Here, geisha shuffle down alleyways, temples enchant visitors and traditional tea shops are scattered about.

Kinkaku-ji

Daitoku-ji

Ginkaku-ji

Nijō-jō

Nanzen-ji

Nishiki Market

Chion-in

Gion

Kiyomizu-dera

Fushimi Inari-Taisha

Osaka Neighbourhoods

Kita (p143)
The working heart of the city, skyscraper-filled Kita is the transport and business hub of Osaka, with some good shopping, shrines and the art museum hidden in amongst the bustle.

⊙ *Osaka-jō*

Dōtombori ⊙

Minami (p125)
The antidote to straight-laced Kita, this is where Osakans come to let their hair down amid flashing neon, late-night bars and some of the city's best shopping arcades.

Explore
Kyoto & Osaka

Kyoto

Kyoto's Walking Tours

Osaka

Osaka's Walking Tour

Riverboat, Arashiyama (p122) GUITAR PHOTOGRAPHER/SHUTTERSTOCK ©

Explore ◉
Kyoto Station & South Kyoto

Dominated by Kyoto Station, this neighbourhood serves as the gateway to Kyoto. There are a couple of temples within walking distance of the station, and the Kyoto Railway Museum is a short bus ride away. Further south is the Shintō shrine complex Fushimi Inari-Taisha, as well as the superb Tōfuku-ji temple and garden.

The Short List

○ **Fushimi Inari-Taisha (p36)** *Wandering through the hypnotic arcades of torii (entrance gates to a Shintō shrine).*

○ **Kyoto Station (p40)** *Gazing up at the striking architecture and taking in views from the Sky Garden.*

○ **Kyoto Tower (p42)** *Whisking up to the top of the tower for great views over the city.*

○ **Nishi Hongan-ji (p41)** *Immersing yourself in the grandeur of this temple.*

○ **Tōfuku-ji (p40)** *Strolling through the expansive grounds of this beautiful temple complex.*

Getting There & Around

🚄 The JR lines, including the *shinkansen* (bullet train), and the private Kintetsu line operate to/from Kyoto Station.

🚌 Many city buses, JR buses and other bus lines operate to/from the Kyoto Station Bus Terminal (on the north side of the station).

Ⓢ The Karasuma subway line stops directly underneath Kyoto Station (the Kyoto Station stop is called simply 'Kyoto').

Kyoto Station & South Kyoto Map on p38

Top Sight

Fushimi Inari-Taisha

With seemingly endless arcades of vermilion torii *spread across a thickly wooded mountain, this vast shrine complex is a world unto itself. It is, quite simply, one of the most impressive and memorable sights in all of Kyoto. A pathway wanders 4km up the mountain and is lined with dozens of atmospheric subshrines.*

MAP P38, G6

伏見稲荷大社

68 Yabunouchi-chō, Fukakusa, Fushimi-ku

admission free

dawn-dusk

JR Nara line to Inari or Keihan line to Fushimi-Inari

From 8th-Century Beginnings

Fushimi Inari-Taisha was dedicated to the gods of rice and sake by the Hata family in the 8th century. As the role of agriculture diminished, deities were enrolled to ensure prosperity in business. Nowadays the shrine is one of Japan's most popular, and is the head shrine for some 40,000 Inari shrines scattered the length and breadth of the country.

The Messenger of Inari

As you explore the shrine, you will come across hundreds of stone foxes. The fox is considered the messenger of Inari, the god of cereals, and the stone foxes, too, are often referred to as Inari. The key often seen in the fox's mouth is for the rice granary. On an incidental note, the Japanese traditionally see the fox as a sacred, somewhat mysterious figure capable of 'possessing' humans – the favoured point of entry is under the fingernails.

Hiking

The walk around the upper precincts of the shrine is a pleasant day hike. It also makes for a very eerie stroll in the late afternoon and early evening, when the various graveyards and miniature shrines along the path take on a mysterious air. It's best to go with a friend at this time.

★ Top Tips

o The shrine is one of the most popular sights in Kyoto, so visit early or late in the day for fewer crowds.

o A good time to visit is in the first few days of January to see thousands of believers visit this shrine as their *hatsu-mōde* (first shrine visit of the New Year) to pray for good fortune.

o Come on 8 April to witness the Sangyō-sai festival, when offerings are made and dances performed to ensure prosperity for national industry.

✕ Take a Break

The Vermillion Espresso Bar (p44) is the perfect place to take a rest after exploring the shrine complex. It serves excellent coffee and cakes.

SHIMABARA

Nishi Hongan-ji 5

Shōmen-dōri

Higashi Hongan-ji

Higashinakasuji-dōri

Shichijō-dōri

Omiya-dōri

Horikawa-dōri

Shichijō-dōri

Kitsuyabashi-dōri

Kyoto Railway Museum 6

Umekōji-kōen

Bicycle Parking Lot

Kyoto Cycling Tour Project

Shiokōji-dōri

JR Iset

11 9

12 15 10

Kyoto

Hachijō-dōri

Kintetsu Kyoto

Inokuma-dōri

Harikoji-dōri

Omiya-dōri

18

Tō-ji 3

16

Tōji-dōri

Tōji

Kujō-dōri

Aburanokōji-dōri

Kyoto Brewing Company

MINAMI-KU

Jūjō

Jujo-dōri

N 0   400 m
   0   0.2 miles

Kamitoba Park

Omiya-dōri

For reviews see
◎ Top Sights   p36
◎ Sights   p40
✕ Eating   p42
🍺 Drinking   p43
🔒 Shopping   p44

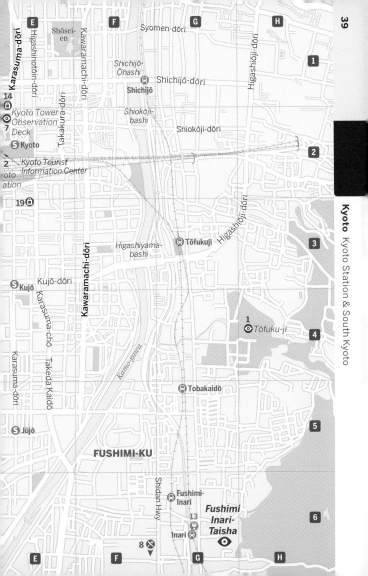

E **F** **G** **H**

Karasuma-dōri

Higashinotōin-dōri

Shōsei-en

Kawaramachi-dōri

Kawaramachi-dōri

Syomen-dōri

Higashiōji-dōri

1

Shichijō-Ōhashi

Shichijō-dōri

Shichijō

Takakura-dōri

Shiokōji-bashi

Shiokōji-dōri

14

Kyoto Tower
Observation
Deck
7

2

Kyoto

2
Kyoto Tourist
Information Center
...oto
...ation

19

Higashiōji-dōri

Higashiyama-
bashi

Tōfukuji

Kawaramachi-dōri

3

Kujō

Kujō-dōri

Karasuma-chō

1
Tōfuku-ji

4

Karasuma-dōri

Takeda Kaidō

Kamo-gawa

Tobakaidō

Jūjō

5

FUSHIMI-KU

Shidan Hwy

Fushimi-
Inari

13

Fushimi
Inari-
Taisha

6

8

Inari

E **F** **G** **H**

Sights

Tōfuku-ji

BUDDHIST TEMPLE

1 ◉ MAP P38, H4

Home to a spectacular garden, several superb structures and beautiful precincts, Tōfuku-ji is one of the best temples in Kyoto. It is linked to Fushimi Inari-Taisha by the Keihan and JR train lines. The present temple complex includes 24 subtemples. The huge **San-mon** is the oldest Zen main gate in Japan, the **Hōjō** (Abbot's Hall) was reconstructed in 1890, and the gardens were laid out in 1938. (東福寺; ☏075-561-0087; www.tofukuji.jp; 15-778 Honmahi, Higashiyama-ku; Hōjō garden ¥400, Tsūten-kyō bridge ¥400; ◷9am-4pm; ℝKeihan or JR Nara line to Tōfukuji)

Kyoto Station

NOTABLE BUILDING

2 ◉ MAP P38, E2

The Kyoto Station building is a striking steel-and-glass structure – a kind of futuristic cathedral for the transport age – with a tremendous space that arches above you as you enter the main concourse. Be sure to take the escalator from the 7th floor on the east side of the building up to the 11th-floor glass corridor, Skyway (open 10am to 10pm), which runs high above the main concourse of the station, and catch some views from the 15th-floor Sky Garden terrace. (京都駅; www.kyoto-station-building.co.jp; Karasuma-dōri, Higashishiokōji-chō, Shiokōji-sagaru, Shimogyō-ku; ℝKyoto Station)

Tō-ji

BUDDHIST TEMPLE

3 ◉ MAP P38, B3

Tō-ji is an appealing complex of halls and a fantastic pagoda that makes a fine backdrop for the monthly flea market held on the grounds. The temple was established in 794 by imperial decree to protect the city. In 823 the emperor handed it over to Kūkai (known posthumously as Kōbō Daishi), the founder of the Shingon school of Buddhism. (東寺; www.toji.or.jp; 1 Kujō-chō, Minami-ku; ¥800, grounds free; ◷8.30am-5pm mid-Apr–mid-Sep, to 4.30pm rest of year; ℝKyoto City bus 205 from Kyoto Station, ℝKintetsu Kyoto line to Tōji)

Higashi Hongan-ji

BUDDHIST TEMPLE

4 ◉ MAP P38, D1

Higashi Hongan-ji is the last word in all things grand and gaudy. Considering its proximity to the station, free admission, awesome structures and dazzling interiors, this temple is the obvious spot to visit when near the station. The temple is dominated by the vast **Goei-dō** (Main Hall), said to be the second-largest wooden structure in Japan, standing 38m high, 76m long and 58m wide. An audio guide (¥500) is available at the information centre. (東本願寺, Eastern Temple of the True Vow; www.higashihonganji.or.jp; Karasuma-dōri, Shichijō-agaru, Shimogyō-ku; admission free; ◷5.50am-5.30pm Mar-Oct, 6.20am-4.30pm Nov-Feb; ℝKyoto Station)

Nishi Hongan-ji BUDDHIST TEMPLE

5 ⊙ MAP P38, C1

A vast temple complex, Nishi Hongan-ji comprises several buildings that feature some of the finest examples of architecture and artistic achievement from the Azuchi-Momoyama period (1568–1603). The **Goei-dō** is a marvellous sight. Another must-see building is the **Daisho-in** hall, which has sumptuous paintings, carvings and metal ornamentation. A small garden and two *nō* (stylised Japanese dance-drama) stages are connected with the hall. The dazzling **Kara-mon** has intricate ornamental carvings. (西本願寺; Horikawa-dōri, Hanayachō-sagaru, Shimogyō-ku; admission free; ⊙5.30am-5pm; 🚉Kyoto Station)

Kyoto Railway Museum MUSEUM

6 ⊙ MAP P38, A2

This superb museum is spread over three floors showcasing 53 trains, from vintage steam locomotives to commuter trains and the first *shinkansen*, from 1964. Kids will love the interactive displays and impressive railroad diorama, with miniature trains zipping through the intricate landscape. You can also take a 10-minute ride on one of the trains (adult/child ¥300/100). (梅小路蒸気機関車館; www.kyotorailwaymuseum.jp; Kankiji-chō, Shimogyō-ku; adult ¥1200, child ¥200-500; ⊙10am-5.30pm, closed Wed; 🚻; 🚉Kyoto City bus 103, 104 or 110 from Kyoto Station to Umekōji-kōen/Kyoto Railway Museum-mae)

East Garden at Tōfuku-ji

Kyoto Tower Observation Deck

VIEWPOINT

7 👁 MAP P38, E2

Located opposite Kyoto Station, this retro tower (1964) looks like a rocket perched atop the Kyoto Tower Hotel. The observation deck provides excellent views in all directions and you can really get a sense of the Kyoto *bonchi* (flat basin). It's a great place to get oriented to the city upon arrival. There are free mounted binoculars to use and a cool touch screen information panel showing what the view looks like both day and night. (京都タワー; Karasuma-dōri, Shichijō-sagaru, Shimogyō-ku; adult ¥770, child ¥150-520; ⏰9am-9pm; 🚉Kyoto Station)

Eating

Vegans Cafe & Restaurant

VEGAN, JAPANESE ¥

8 🍴 MAP P38, F6

Who needs meat and dairy when food can taste this good without them? This light-filled cafe is a haven for vegans and vegetarians, with a range of meals from healthy salad, rice and miso sets, to huge bowls of soy-milk miso ramen and deep-fried tofu pizza. There's organic beer, wine and coffee, too. It's a convenient detour when sightseeing around Fushimi-Inari. (📞075-643-3922; www.veganscafe. com; 4-88 Nishiura-chō, Fukakusa, Fushimi-ku; meals ¥540-2500; ⏰11.30am-5pm Thu-Tue, to 9pm Sat; 🛜🌱; 🚉Keihan line to Fujinomori)

Kyoto Rāmen Kōji

RAMEN ¥

9 🍴 MAP P38, D2

If you love ramen, do not miss this collection of nine ramen restaurants on the 10th floor of the Kyoto Station building (on the west end, take the escalators that start in the main concourse, or access via the JR Isetan Department Store south elevator to the 11th floor). Buy tickets from the machines (in English, with pictures) before queuing. (京都拉麺小路; 📞075-361-4401; www.kyoto-ramen-koji.com; 10fl Kyoto Station Bldg, Karasuma-dōri, Shiokōji-sagaru, Shimogyō-ku; ramen ¥840-1250; ⏰11am-10pm; 🚉Kyoto Station)

First Impressions

👀

Odds are, your first step in Kyoto will be onto one of the train platforms in Kyoto Station. This being the case, be warned that your first glimpse of the city is likely to be an anticlimax as the area around the station is mainly concrete, malls and hotels, with the retro Kyoto Tower dominating the landscape. But, rest assured, there is good stuff (and the more traditional landscape you probably came here for) in every direction.

Kyoto Tower Sando

FOOD HALL ¥

Head to the basement floor of the Kyoto Tower building (see 7 ⊙ Map p38, E2) for a range of food stalls to feast at. There's everything from a Mexican taco stand and ramen to *yakiniku* (grilled meat) and *kaiten-sushi* (conveyor-belt sushi). Seek out stand-up bar Roots of all Evil (p44) for a pre- or postdinner gin cocktail. (www.kyoto-tower-sando. jp; Kyoto Tower, B1 Karasuma-dōri, Shichijō-sagaru, Shimogyō-ku; ⊙11am-11pm; ◪Kyoto Station)

Eat Paradise

JAPANESE ¥

10 🍴 MAP P38, D2

On the 10th floor of the Kyoto Station building, you'll find this collection of decent restaurants. Among the choices here are Tonkatsu Wako for *tonkatsu* (deep-fried breaded pork cutlet), Tenichi for sublime tempura, and Wakuden for approachable *kaiseki* (Japanese haute cuisine). (イートパラダイス; ☎075-352-1111; 10F Kyoto Station Bldg, Karasuma-dōri, Shiokōji-sagaru, Shimogyō-ku; ⊙11am-10pm; ◪Kyoto Station)

Cube

JAPANESE ¥

11 🍴 MAP P38, D2

This is a great collection of restaurants located on the 10th floor of the Kyoto Station building; otherwise it can be accessed by the JR Isetan Department Store south elevator (11th floor). Most of the restaurants here serve

Kyoto Brewing Company

You'll find the Kyoto Brewing Company's beer in many of Kyoto's bars, but it's worth a trip out to its **tasting room** (京都醸造株式会社; Map p38, B4; ☎075-574-7820; www.kyoto-brewing.com; 25-1 Takahata-chō, Nishikujō, Minami-ku; ⊙noon-6pm Sat & Sun; ◪Kintetsu line to Jūjō) to sample it in a friendly, local setting in South Kyoto. Check out the brewery vats as you sip on a selection of 10 beers on tap, including a few seasonal releases. Open most weekends; check the website for the schedule.

Japanese food and some come with views. Note the restaurants can get crowded with queues, especially on weekends. (ザ キューブ; ☎075-371-2134; 10F Kyoto Station Bldg, Karasuma-dōri, Shiokōji-sagaru, Shimogyō-ku; ⊙11am-10pm; ◪Kyoto Station)

Drinking

Kurasu

COFFEE

12 ☕ MAP P38, D2

Finally there's good coffee to be found near Kyoto Station! This minimalist cafe has a menu of monthly rotating coffee from speciality roasters in Japan, and offers filter coffee and espresso along with a *matcha* latte and Prana chai. (☎075-744-0804; www.

kurasu.kyoto; 552 Higashiaburano-koji chō, Shimogyō-ku; ⊙8am-6pm; 🛜; 🚉Kyoto Station)

Vermillion Espresso Bar   CAFE

13 🚇 MAP P38, G6

A Melbourne-inspired cafe, tiny Vermillion takes its name from the colour of the *torii* of the nearby Fushimi Inari-Taisha shrine. It does standout coffee as well as a small selection of cakes, which can be taken away or enjoyed at the communal table. It's on the main street, just a short hop from Inari Station. (バーミリオン; www.vermillioncafe.com; 85 Onmae-chō, Fukakusa-inari, Fushimi-ku; ⊙9am-5pm; 🛜; 🚉JR Nara line to Inari or Keihan line to Fushimi-Inari)

Roots of all Evil   BAR

Stop by this standing bar in the Kyoto Tower Sando (see 7 ◉ Map p38, E2) food basement for creative gin cocktails. It's run by the owner of Nokishita 711 (p61) and offers

---

interesting herbal, spicy, floral gin infusions. Cocktails from ¥800. (www.nokishita.net; Kyoto Tower, B1 Karasuma-dōri, Shichijō-sagaru, Shimogyō-ku; ⊙11am-11pm; 🚉Kyoto Station)

Shopping

Yodobashi Camera   ELECTRONICS

14 🔒 MAP P38, E1

This mammoth shop sells a range of electronics, cameras and computer goods, and also has a restaurant floor, a branch of popular budget clothing store Uniqlo, a supermarket, a bookshop, a cafe and, well, the list goes on. It's a few minutes' walk north of Kyoto Station. You can buy travel SIM cards here, too. (ヨドバシカメラ; 📞075-351-1010; 590-2 Higashi Shiokōji-chō, Shimogyō-ku; ⊙9.30am-10pm, restaurants 11am-11pm; 🚉Kyoto Station)

Bic Camera   ELECTRONICS

15 🔒 MAP P38, D2

The sheer number of gadgets and goods this shop has on display is amazing. Just be sure that an English operating manual is available for your purchase. It's also a good place to pick up a prepaid Japanese SIM card. It's directly connected to Kyoto Station via the Nishinotō-in gate; otherwise, it's accessed by leaving the north (Karasuma) gate and walking west. (ビックカメラ; 📞075-353-1111; 927 Higashi Shiokōji-chō, Shimogyō-ku; ⊙10am-9pm; 🚉Kyoto Station)

Hailing a Taxi in High Season

During high seasons for tourism (cherry-blossom season in April and autumn-foliage season in November), the queues at the taxi ranks on the south and north side of Kyoto Station can be very long. If you're in a hurry, walk a few blocks north of the station and hail a cab off the street.

Kōbō-san Market
MARKET

16 MAP P38, B3

This monthly market is held at Tō-ji to commemorate the death of Kōbō Daishi, who in 823 was appointed abbot of the temple. If you're after used kimonos, pottery, bric-a-brac, plants, tools and general Japanalia, this is the place. (弘法さん, 東寺露天市; 1 Kujō-chō, Tō-ji, Minami-ku; ⏱21st of each month; 🚌Kyoto City bus 205 from Kyoto Station, 🚉Kintetsu Kyoto line to Tōji)

Kōjitsu Sansō
SPORTS & OUTDOORS

17 MAP P38, E1

On the 5th floor of the Yodobashi Camera building, this is one of Kyoto's biggest outdoor goods shops. If you're heading up to the Japan Alps to do some hiking, you might want to stop here before getting on the train. (好日山荘; 📞075-708-5178; 5th fl, Kyoto Yodobashi Camera, 590-2 Higashi Shiokōji-chō, Shimogyō-ku; ⏱9.30am-10pm; 🚉Kyoto Station)

Æon Mall Kyoto
SHOPPING CENTRE

18 MAP P38, D3

A five-minute walk southwest of Kyoto Station (exit Hachijō-guchi), you'll find branches of most of the big Japanese retailers here, including Muji, Uniqlo and Sofmap (computers etc). There's

Last-Minute Gifts

Isetan (ジェイアール京都伊勢丹; Map p38, D2; 📞075-352-1111; Kyoto Station Bldg, Karasuma-dōri, Shiokōji-sagaru, Shimogyō-ku; ⏱10am-8pm; 🚉Kyoto Station) is an elegant department store located inside the Kyoto Station building, making it perfect for a last-minute spot of shopping before hopping on the train to the airport or your next destination. Don't miss the B1 and B2 food floors.

a supermarket on the 1st floor and you'll find a food floor, cinema and arcade games on the 4th floor. (イオンモール; 1 Nishikujō Toriiguchi-chō, Minami-ku; ⏱10am-9pm, food floor to 10pm; 🚉Kyoto Station)

Avanti
DEPARTMENT STORE

19 MAP P38, E3

While this mall doesn't offer much of interest, there is a decent selection of restaurants and a food court. It's geared mostly to younger Kyoto shoppers, but it's good for browsing if you have time to kill while waiting for a train. Take the underground passage from Kyoto Station. (アバンティ; 📞075-682-5031; Higashikujō Nishisannō-chō 31, Minami-ku; ⏱10am-9pm, restaurants 11am-10pm; 🚉Kyoto Station)

Explore 🧭
Downtown Kyoto

If all you're interested in on your Kyoto trip is dining on great cuisine, knocking back sake and craft beer at bars, boutique shopping and staying in some of the finest ryokan, you may just never leave Downtown Kyoto (which is, naturally, smack bang in the middle of the city). And you wouldn't need to sacrifice culture or sightseeing, with heavyweight attractions such as Nijō-jō, the famed Nishiki Market and a smattering of small temples, shrines and museums.

The Short List

○ **Nijō-jō (p50)** Treading lightly over squeaking 'night-ingale' floors while exploring the castle.

○ **Nishiki Market (p48)** Marvelling at all the weird and wonderful ingredients that go into Kyoto cuisine.

○ **Ponto-chō (p56)** Strolling this atmospheric street in the evening lantern light.

○ **Takashimaya (p63)** Drooling over the gourmet goods on display in this department store's basement food floor.

Getting There & Around

S The Karasuma subway line stops at Shijō and Karasuma-Oike Stations. The Tōzai line also stops at Karasuma-Oike Station and Kyoto-Shiyakusho-mae Station.

🚃 The Hankyū line stops at Karasuma and Kawaramachi Stations.

🚌 Many city buses stop in Downtown Kyoto.

Downtown Kyoto Map on p54

Top Sight 📷
Nishiki Market

Nishiki Market (Nishiki-kōji Ichiba) is one of Kyoto's real highlights, especially if you have an interest in cooking and eating. Commonly known as Kyoto no daidokoro (Kyoto's kitchen) by locals, it's where most of Kyoto's high-end restaurateurs and well-to-do do their food shopping. This is the place to see the weird and wonderful foods that go into Kyoto cuisine.

◎ MAP P54, F4

錦市場

Nishikikōji-dōri, btwn Teramachi & Takakura, Nakagyō-ku

🕑 9am-5pm

🆂 Karasuma line to Shijō, 🚃 Hankyū line to Karasuma or Kawaramachi

History

The pedestrian-only, covered Nishiki Market is right in the centre of town, one block north of Shijō-dōri, running from Teramachi *shōtengai* (market streets) to Takakura-dōri (ending almost behind Daimaru department store). It's said that there were shops here as early as the 14th century, and it's known for sure that the street was a wholesale fish market in the Edo period (1603–1868). After the end of Edo, as Japan entered the modern era, the market became a retail market, which it remains today.

The Wares

The emphasis is on locally produced Japanese food items such as *tsukemono* (Japanese pickles), tea, beans, rice, seaweed and fish. In recent years the market has been evolving from a strictly local food market into a tourist attraction, and you'll now find several shops selling Kyoto-style souvenirs mixed in among the food stalls.

Shopping Highlight

Aritsugu (p63) turns out some of the most exquisite knives on earth. Take time to pick the perfect one for your needs, then watch as the artisans carefully put a final edge on the knife with a giant round sharpening stone – the end product will be so sharp it will scare you.

★ Top Tips

o The market is quite narrow and can get elbow-to-elbow busy, so try visiting early or later in the afternoon if you prefer a bit of space.

o Some shops don't appreciate visitors taking photos, so it's a good idea to ask politely before snapping away.

✕ Take a Break

o Drop in to Nishiki Warai (p59) for a tasty *okonomiyaki* (savoury pancake) lunch.

o Queue up for some of the city's best ramen just steps from the market at Ippūdō (p60).

Top Sight 📷
Nijō-jō

Standing like a direct challenge to the might of the emperor in the nearby Imperial Palace, the shogun castle of Nijō-jō is a stunning monument to the power of the warlords who effectively ruled Japan for centuries. It's a fascinating destination, with superb (almost rococo) interiors, and the grounds contain expansive gardens which are perfect for a stroll.

◎ MAP P54, B1

二条城

541 Nijōjō-chō, Nijō-dōri, Horikawa nishi-iru, Nakagyō-ku

adult/child ¥600/200

🕐 8.45am–5pm, last entry 4pm, closed Tue Dec, Jan, Jul & Aug

Ⓢ Tōzai line to Nijō-jō-mae, Ⓡ JR line to Nijō

Background

Nijō-jō is built on land that was originally occupied by the 8th-century Imperial Palace,
which was abandoned in 1227. The castle
was constructed in 1603 as the official Kyoto
residence of the first Tokugawa shogun, Ieyasu.
To safeguard against treachery, Ieyasu had the
interior fitted with 'nightingale' floors (intruders
were detected by the squeaking boards) and
concealed chambers where bodyguards could
keep watch and spring out at a moment's notice.

In 1868 the last Tokugawa shogun, Yosh-
inobu, surrendered his power to the newly
restored Emperor Meiji inside Nijō-jō.

The Shinsen-en Garden, just south of the castle, is all that remains of the original palace. This
forlorn garden has small shrines and a pond.

Highlights

The **Momoyama-era Kara-mon gate**, originally
part of Hideyoshi's Fushimi-jō in the south of
the city, features masterful woodcarving and
metalwork. After passing through the gate, you
enter the **Ninomaru palace**, which is divided
into five buildings with numerous chambers.
Access to the buildings used to depend on rank
– only those of highest rank were permitted
into the inner buildings. The **Ōhiroma Yon-no-
Ma** (Fourth Chamber) has spectacular screen
paintings, though these are reproductions.
Original paintings are stored in the **Nijo Castle
400th Anniversary Gallery**.

The neighbouring **Honmaru palace** dates
from the mid-19th century. After the Meiji Restoration in 1868, the castle became a detached
palace of the imperial household and in 1939 it
was given to Kyoto City.

Ninomaru Palace Garden, which surrounds
the inner castle buildings, is a must-see. It
was designed by Kobori Enshū, Japan's most
celebrated garden designer. The vast garden
comprises three separate islets spanned by
stone bridges and is meticulously maintained.

★ Top Tips

o The castle is on
the itinerary of every
foreign and Japanese
tour group and it
can be packed. If
you're after peace
and quiet, try an
early-morning or
late-afternoon visit.

o To get more out of
your visit, you can
hire an audio guide
for ¥500 or go on an
English guided tour
for ¥2000.

o Honmaru palace is
only open for special
autumn viewing.

o Nijo Castle gallery
exhibitions change
quarterly and are
on display during
scheduled periods
throughout the year
(check the website
for the schedule).

o The Ninomaru
palace and garden
take about an hour
to walk through (a
detailed fact sheet in
English is provided).

✕ Take a Break

o Tuck into a home-
made vegie burger,
vegan cake and
single-origin coffee at
Cafe Phalam (p59).

Walking Tour 🚶

Shop till You Drop

This area is Kyoto's beating heart of consumerism, where locals head to shop at the best boutiques and departments stores, pick up gourmet goods from the Nishiki Market to cook at home, and stop off for a casual lunch and coffee in between.

Walk Facts

Start Nishiki Market

End Ippōdō Tea

Length 2.5km; two to three hours

❶ Nishiki Market

Arrive early to beat the crowds at this wonderful market (p48), home to a bounty of ingredients that go into Kyoto's cuisine. Wander from stall to stall inspecting the gourmet goods, duck into shops selling spices and sweets, and grab a snack to go.

❷ Daimaru

You can really while away the hours at Daimaru (p65), perhaps Japan's best-known department store. Most of that time could be spent just checking out what's on offer in the basement food section, where locals head to pick up *bentō* boxes, sweets, tempura and sushi.

❸ Takashimaya

Takashimaya (p63) department store is a favourite for the wide variety of quality goods on offer. Take your time here moving from floor to floor, browsing everything from pottery, kimonos and lacquerware to fashion, homewares and the fantastic basement food floors.

❹ Tagoto Honten

Take a break at **Tagoto Honten** (田ごと本店; ☎075-221-1811; www. kyoto-tagoto.co.jp; 34 Otabi-chō, Shijō-dōri, Kawaramachi nishi-iru, Nakagyō-ku; lunch/dinner from ¥1850/6000; ⏰11.30am-3pm & 4.30-9pm; 🚆Keihan line to Shijō or Hankyū line to Kawaramachi), a magnet for shoppers in need of a feed. It's a great spot to sample affordable *kaiseki* (Japanese haute cuisine) in a lovely, quiet setting that has you forgetting the hustle of the main streets outside. Save room for dessert, though.

❺ Karafuneya Coffee Sanjō Honten

Karafuneya (からふねや珈琲三条本店; ☎075-254-8774; 39 Daikoku-chō, Kawaramachi-dōri, Sanjō-sagaru, Nakagyō-ku; parfaits from ¥780; ⏰9am-11pm, to 1am Fri & Sat; Ⓢ Tōzai line to Kyoto-Shiyakusho-mae, 🚆Keihan line to Sanjō) is a local's favourite for light lunches and coffee, but the real temptation is the huge selection of sundaes on the menu. Tuck into a *matcha* (powdered green tea) parfait or *azuki* (sweet red bean) with black sesame.

❻ Kaboku Tearoom

Make your way to these lovely **tearooms** (喫茶室嘉木; Teramachi-dōri, Nijō-agaru, Nakagyō-ku; ⏰10am-6pm; Ⓢ Tōzai line to Kyoto-Shiyakusho-mae) to refresh yourself with a cup of tea. Choose from a range of green teas, and watch the *matcha* being whisked up at the counter.

❼ Ippōdō Tea

Head to Ippōdō Tea (p64) to stock up on tea to take home. Bags and small containers make the perfect lightweight souvenir of your shopping day.

Nijō-jō

Nijō-jō-mae Ⓢ

Shinsen'en

Oike-dōri

Aneyakōji-dōri

Sanjō-dōri

Rokkaku-dōri

Koin-dōri

Takoyakushi-dōri

Nishikikōji-dōri

Ōmiya

Shijō-dōri

Shijō-Ōmiya

Takatsuji-dōri

Manjuji-dōri

NAKAGYŌ-KU

Horikawa-dōri

Aburanokōji-dōri

Ogawa-dōri

Kamaza-dōri

Shinmachi-dōri

Senbon-dōri

Mibu-dōri

Omiya-dōri

Kuromon-dōri

Horikawa-dōri

Nishinotōin-dōri

Shinmachi-dōri

Oshikōji-dōri

⊗13

15◎

For reviews see

Ⓝ 0 ___ 400 m
0 ___ 0.2 miles

Sights

Ponto-chō
AREA

1 🎯 MAP P54, H3

There are few streets in Asia this atmospheric. The narrow street comes alive at night, with wonderful lanterns, traditional wooden exteriors, and elegant Kyotoites disappearing into the doorways of elite old restaurants and bars. (先斗町; Ponto-chō, Nakagyō-ku; Ⓢ Tōzai line to Sanjō-Keihan or Kyoto-Shiyakusho-mae, Ⓡ Keihan line to Sanjō, Hankyū line to Kawaramachi)

Kyoto Ukiyo-e
MUSEUM

2 🎯 MAP P54, G4

Opened in 2017, this one-room museum displays a selection of *ukiyo-e* (woodblock prints) by some of Japan's most well-known artists, including Hiroshige Utagawa, Utamaro Kitagawa and Hokusai Katsushika. *Ukiyo-e* is said to have originated in the 16th century with prints showing the lives of common people in Kyoto, and most of the works shown here are of scenes from Kyoto. The exhibitions change every few months but Japan's most famous *ukiyo-e* work, Hokusai's *The Great Wave off Kanagawa*, is permanently on display. (京都浮世絵美術館; 📞 075-223-3003; www.kyoto-ukiyoe-museum.com; 2nd fl, Kirihata Bldg, Shijō-dōri, Teramachi Nishiiri, Shimogyō-ku; adult/child ¥1000/300; ⏰ 10.30am-6.30pm; Ⓡ Hankyū line to Kawaramachi)

Kyoto International Manga Museum
MUSEUM

3 🎯 MAP P54, E2

Located in an old elementary school building, this museum is the perfect introduction to the art of manga (Japanese comics). It has 300,000 manga in its collection, 50,000 of which are on display in the *Wall of Manga* exhibit. While most of the manga and displays are in Japanese, the collection of translated works is growing. In addition to the galleries that show both the historical development of manga and original artwork done in manga style, there are beginners' workshops and portrait drawings on weekends. (京都国際マンガミュージアム; www.kyotomm.jp; Karasuma-dōri, Oike-agaru, Nakagyō-ku; adult/child

Artist at Kyoto International Manga Museum

¥800/100; ⏱10am-6pm Tue-Thu;
🎎; Ⓢ Karasuma or Tōzai lines to
Karasuma-Oike)

Museum of Kyoto MUSEUM

4 ◉ MAP P54, F3

This museum is worth visiting
if a special exhibition is on (the
regular exhibits are not particularly
interesting and don't have much in
the way of English explanations).
Check the *Kyoto Visitor's Guide*
for upcoming special exhibitions.
On the 1st floor, the Roji Tempō
is a reconstruction of a typical
merchant area in Kyoto during the
Edo period (this section can be entered free; some of the shops sell
souvenirs and serve local dishes).
(京都文化博物館; 📞075-222-0888;
www.bunpaku.or.jp; Takakura-dōri,
Sanjō-agaru, Nakagyō-ku; adult/child
¥500/free, extra for special exhibitions;
⏱10am-7.30pm Tue-Sun; Ⓢ Karasuma
or Tōzai lines to Karasuma-Oike)

Eating

Honke Owariya NOODLES ¥

5 🍴 MAP P54, E2

Set in an old sweet shop in a
traditional Japanese building on
a quiet downtown street, this is
where locals come for excellent
soba (buckwheat-noodle) dishes.
The highly recommended house
speciality, *hourai soba* (¥2160),
comes with a stack of five small
plates of soba with a selection of
toppings, including shiitake mush-
rooms, shrimp tempura, thin slices
of omelette and sesame seeds.

Where to Go for Breakfast? 🍴

Simple and **Apprivoiser
Wholefood Cafe** (Map p54, G6;
📞075-351-6251; http://vegecafe.
org; 716 Kawaramachi-dōri,
Matsubara-sagaru, Shimogyō-ku;
meals from ¥500; ⏱8am-7pm
Tue-Sun; 📶🍴; 🚉Hankyū line
to Kawaramachi or Keihan line to
Kiyomizu-Gojō) is a great spot
to grab a healthy breakfast – it
opens early (a rarity in Kyoto)
and serves a tasty, cheap
Japanese breakfast set, a good
morning curry and homemade
granola with yoghurt, along
with organic coffee and a delicious house-made chai.

(本家尾張屋; 📞075-231-3446; www.
honke-owariya.co.jp; 322 Kurumaya-
chō, Nijō, Nakagyō-ku; dishes from
¥810; ⏱11am-7pm; Ⓢ Karasuma or
Tōzai lines to Karasuma-Oike)

Roan Kikunoi KAISEKI ¥¥¥

6 🍴 MAP P54, H4

Roan Kikunoi is a fantastic place
to experience the wonders of
kaiseki. It's a lovely intimate space
located right downtown. The chef
takes an experimental and creative
approach and the results are a
wonder for the eyes and palate.
Highly recommended. Reserve
through your hotel or ryokan,
at least a few days in advance.
(露庵菊乃井; 📞075-361-5580; www.
kikunoi.jp; 118 Saito-chō, Kiyamachi-
dōri, Shijō-sagaru, Shimogyō-ku;

lunch/dinner from ¥7000/13,000; ⏱11.30am-1.30pm & 5-8.30pm Thu-Tue; 🚉Hankyū line to Kawaramachi or Keihan line to Gion-Shijō)

Yoshikawa TEMPURA ¥¥¥

7 ✕ MAP P54, F2

This is the place to go for delectable tempura with a daily changing menu. Attached to the **Yoshikawa ryokan** (吉川; s/d from ¥50,000/54,000; ❄ @ 🛜), it offers table seating, but it's much more interesting to sit and eat around the small intimate counter and observe the chefs at work. Reservation is required for the private tatami room or counter bar for dinner. Note: counter bar is closed Sunday. (吉川; 📞075-221-5544; www.kyoto-yoshikawa.co.jp; 135 Matsushita-chō, Tominokōji, Oike-sagaru, Nakagyō-ku; lunch ¥3000-25,000, dinner ¥8000-25,000; ⏱11am-1.45pm & 5-8pm; Ⓢ Tōzai line to Karasuma-Oike or Kyoto-Shiyakusho-mae)

Giro Giro Hitoshina KAISEKI ¥¥

8 ✕ MAP P54, G6

Giro Giro takes traditional *kaiseki* and strips it of any formality, so you're left with great food in a boisterous atmosphere and with thousands more yen in your pocket. In a quiet lane near Kiyamachi-dōri, things liven up inside with patrons sitting at the counter around the open kitchen, chatting with chefs preparing inventive dishes. (📞075-343-7070; 420-7 Nanba-chō, Nishi-kiyamachi-

dōri, Matsubara-sagaru, Shimogyō-ku; kaiseki ¥4100; ⏱5.30pm-midnight; 🚉Hankyū line to Kawaramachi or Keihan line to Kiyomizu-Gojō)

Café Bibliotec Hello! CAFE ¥

9 ✕ MAP P54, F1

As the name suggests, books line the walls of this cool cafe located in a converted *machiya* (traditional town house) attracting a mix of locals and tourists. It's a great place to relax with a book or to tap away at your laptop over a coffee (¥450) or light lunch. Look for the huge banana plants out the front. (カフェビブリオティックハロー！; 📞075-231-8625; 650 Seimei-chō, Nijō-dōri, Yanaginobanba higashi-iru, Nakagyō-ku; meals from ¥850; ⏱11.30am-midnight; 🛜; Ⓢ Tōzai line to Kyoto-Shiyakusho-mae)

Menami JAPANESE ¥¥

10 ✕ MAP P54, H3

This welcoming neighbourhood favourite specialises in *obanzai-ryōri* – a type of home-style cooking using seasonal ingredients – done creatively and served as tapas-size plates. Don't miss the delicious spring rolls wrapped with *yuba* (tofu skin; 生ゆば春巻). Try to book a counter seat where you can eye off bowls filled with dishes to choose from while watching the chefs in action. (めなみ; 📞075-231-1095; www.menami.jp; Kiyamachi-dōri, Sanjō-agaru, Nakagyō-ku; dishes ¥400-1600; ⏱5-11pm Mon-Sat; Ⓢ Tōzai line to Kyoto-Shiyakusho-mae, 🚉Keihan line to Sanjō)

Mishima-tei

JAPANESE ¥¥¥

11 ✕ MAP P54, G3

Mishima-tei, around since 1873, is a good place to sample sukiyaki (thin slices of beef cooked in sake, soy and vinegar broth, and dipped in raw egg) as the quality of the meat is very high, which is hardly surprising when there is a butcher downstairs. It's at the intersection of the Sanjō and Teramachi covered arcades. (三嶋亭; 📞 075-221-0003; 405 Sakurano-chō, Teramachi-dōri, Sanjō-sagaru, Nakagyō-ku; sukiyaki lunch/dinner from ¥7720/14,850; ⏱11.30am-10.30pm Thu-Tue; Ⓢ Tōzai line to Kyoto-Shiyakusho-mae)

Tsukiji Sushisei

SUSHI ¥

12 ✕ MAP P54, F4

On the basement floor, next to Daimaru department store, this simple sushi restaurant serves excellent sushi. You can order a set or just point at what looks good. You can see inside the restaurant from street level, so it should be easy to spot. (築地寿司清; 📞 075-252-1537; 581 Obiya-chō, Takakura-dōri, Nishikikōji-sagaru, Nakagyō-ku; sushi sets from ¥1512, per piece from ¥162; ⏱11.30am-3pm & 5-10pm Mon-Fri, 11.30am-10pm Sat & Sun; Ⓢ Karasuma line to Shijō)

Cafe Phalam

CAFE ¥

13 ✕ MAP P54, A2

A short walk from Nijō-jō (p50), this homey cafe is a great spot to lunch on mainly vegan and vegetarian homemade food, from vegie burgers with salad to vegan cakes. The excellent coffee is made from beans sourced from Africa and South America, and

Cheap Eats 🍽

If you've never tried a *kaiten-sushi* (conveyor-belt sushi restaurant), don't miss **Sushi no Musashi** (寿しのむさし; Map p54, G3; 📞075-222-0634; www.sushinomusashi.com; Kawaramachi-dōri, Sanjō-agaru, Nakagyō-ku; plates from ¥146; ⏱11am-10pm; Ⓢ Tōzai line to Kyoto-Shiyakusho-mae, Ⓡ Keihan line to Sanjō). Most dishes are a mere ¥146. Not the best sushi in the world, but it's cheap, reliable and fun. It's also easy to eat here: you just grab what you want off the conveyor belt.

Nishiki Warai (錦わらい; Map p54, F4; 📞075-257-5966; www.nishiki warai.com; 1st fl, Mizukōto Bldg, 597 Nishiuoya-chō, Nishikikōji-dōri, Takakura nishi-iru, Nakagyō-ku; okonomiyaki from ¥700; ⏱11.30am-midnight; Ⓢ Karasuma line to Shijō, Ⓡ Hankyū line to Karasuma) is a great place to try *okonomiyaki* (savoury pancakes) in casual surroundings. Non-smokers might find it a bit smoky at times, but it's a fun spot to eat. Your *okonomiyaki* will be served ready-made to the hotplate at your table. It's about 20m west of the west end of Nishiki Market.

Vegetarian Dining 🍴

Located diagonally across from Nakagyō post office, **Biotei** (びお亭; Map p54, E3; 📞075-255-0086; 2nd fl, M&I Bldg, 28 Umetada-chō, Sanjō-dōri, Higashinotōin nishi-iru, Nakagyō-ku; lunch/dinner sets from ¥890/1385; ⏰11.30am-2pm Tue-Sat, 5-8.30pm Tue-Wed & Fri-Sat; 🍴; Ⓢ Tōzai or Karasuma lines to Karasuma-Oike) is a favourite of Kyoto vegetarians, serving à la carte and daily sets with dishes such as deep-fried crumbed tofu and black seaweed salad with rice, miso and pickles. The seating is rather cramped but the food is excellent, beautifully presented and carefully made from quality ingredients.

Above the mumokuteki shop in the middle of the downtown area, the popular **mumokuteki cafe** (ムモクテキカフェ; Map p54, G3; 📞075-213-7733; www.mumokuteki.com; 2nd fl, Human Forum Bldg, 351 Iseya-chō, Gokomachi-dōri, Rokkaku-sagaru, Nakagyō-ku; meals from ¥1000; ⏰11.30am-9pm; 🍴; 🚈Hankyū line to Kawaramachi) is a lifesaver for many Kyoto vegetarians. The food is tasty, varied and served in casual homey surroundings. Try the tofu and avocado burger paired with a fresh vegetable juice. Most of the food served is vegan.

the kids will be happy with the selection of toys. (カフェパラン; 📞075-496-4843; www.phalam.jp; Shin Nijyo Bldg, 24 Hokusei-chō, Nishinokyo, Nakagyō-ku; meals from ¥850, coffee ¥330; ⏰9am-8pm Mon-Fri, to 7pm Sat & Sun; 🛜🍴; Ⓢ Tōzai line to Nijō, 🚈JR line to Nijō)

Ippūdō
RAMEN ¥

15 🗺 MAP P54, F4

There's a reason that there's usually a line outside this place: the ramen is fantastic and the bite-sized *gyōza* are to die for. The *gyōza* set meal (from ¥1440) is great value. While it's not on the menu, you can request a vegetarian option. (一風堂; 📞075-213-8800; Higashinotō-in, Nishikikōji higashi-iru, Nakagyō-ku; ramen from

¥790; ⏰11am-3am, to 2am Sun; Ⓢ Karasuma line to Shijō)

Drinking

Bungalow
CRAFT BEER

15 📍 MAP P54, C4

Spread over two floors with an open-air downstairs bar, Bungalow serves a great range of Japanese craft beer along with natural wines in a cool industrial space. The regularly changing menu features 10 beers on tap from all over Japan and it also serves excellent food. (バンガロー; 📞075-256-8205; www.bungalow.jp; 15 Kashiwaya-chō, Shijō-dōri, Shimogyō-ku; ⏰3pm-2am Mon-Sat; 🚈Hankyū line to Ōmiya)

Weekenders Coffee COFFEE

16 🚇 MAP P54, F3

Weekenders is a tiny coffee bar tucked away in a traditional-style building at the back of a parking lot. Sure, it's a strange location, but it's where you'll find some of the city's best coffee being brewed by roaster-owner Masahiro Kaneko. It's mostly takeaway with a small bench out front. (ウィークエンダーズ コーヒー; 📞075-746-2206; www.weekenderscoffee.com; 560 Honeyana-chō, Nakagyō-ku; coffee from ¥430; ⏰7.30am-6pm Thu-Tue; 🚉Hankyū line to Kawaramachi)

Bee's Knees COCKTAIL BAR

17 🚇 MAP P54, H4

Speakeasy-style cocktail bars have been popping up of late, and this one hits the mark with its 'secret entrance' (look for the subtle bee sign), pressed metal ceilings, dark wood and dim lighting. Chatty bartenders mix up Prohibition-era classics with a twist – try the *matcha* tiramisu or the smoked mojito with cherry-blossom wood smoke. (📞075-585-5595; www.bees-knees-kyoto.jp; 1st fl, Matsuya Bldg, 364 Kamiya-chō, Nishikiyamachi-dōri, Shijō-agaru, Nakagyō-ku; cocktails from ¥1300; ⏰6pm-1am Mon-Thu, to 2am Fri & Sat; 🚉Keihan line to Gion-Shijō or Hankyū line to Kawaramachi)

Nokishita 711 COCKTAIL BAR

18 🚇 MAP P54, H5

The sign inside says 'Kyoto Loves Gin', and if you do too you won't want to miss this quirky little bar. Owner Tomo infuses gin with interesting ingredients, such as bamboo and smoked tea, and mixes up delicious cocktails with unique flavours. There's a great range of gins from around the world. (📞075-741-6564; www.nokishita.net; 235 Atsumari-B, Sendo-chō, Shimogyō-ku; ⏰6pm-2am, to midnight Sun & Mon; 🛜; 🚉Hankyū line to Kawaramachi)

Kiln COFFEE

19 🚇 MAP P54, H4

On a pretty stretch of canal on scenic Kiyamachi-dōri, Kiln's big windows frame the view and make it the perfect spot to stare lazily while waiting for your caffeine to kick in. The brew is made with single-origin beans and there's a selection of cakes and toasted sandwiches. (📞075-353-3555; 194 Sendo-chō, Kiyamachi-dōri, Shimogyō-ku; ⏰11am-11pm Thu-Tue; 🛜; 🚉Hankyū line to Kawaramachi)

Taigu PUB

20 🚇 MAP P54, H2

Looking out on scenic Kiyamachi-dōri, Taigu (formerly Tadg's Gastro Pub) is a good spot for an evening drink. Choose from an extensive selection of craft beers (including several rotating Japanese beers on tap), a variety of wines, sake and spirits. It also does pub-style meals. (ダイグ ガストロ パブ; 📞075-213-0214; 1st fl, 498 Kamikoriki-chō, Nakagyō-ku; ⏰11.30am-11pm; 🛜; 🚇Tōzai line to Kyoto-Shiyakusho-mae)

Get Schooled on Sake

Sake Bar Yoramu (酒バーよらむ; Map p54, F2; ☎075-213-1512; www.sakebar-yoramu.com; 35-1 Matsuya-chō, Nijō-dōri, Higashinotoin higashi-iru, Nakagyō-ku; ☻6pm-midnight Wed-Sat; Ⓢ Karasuma or Tōzai lines to Karasuma-Oike) is highly recommended for anyone after an education in sake. It's very small and can accommodate onlya handful of people. If you're not sure what you like, go for a sake tasting set of three (¥1700). By day, it's a soba restaurant called Toru Soba.

Bar K6   BAR

21 🚇 MAP P54, H1

Overlooking one of the prettiest stretches of Kiyamachi-dōri, this upscale modern bar has a great selection of single malts and some of the best cocktails in town. It's popular with well-heeled locals and travellers staying at some of the top hotels nearby. (バーK 6; ☎075-255-5009; 2nd fl, Le Valls Bldg, Nijō-dōri, Kiyamachi higashi-iru, Nakagyō-ku; ☻6pm-3am, to 5am Fri & Sat; Ⓢ Tōzai line to Kyoto-Shiyakusho-mae, 🚃 Keihan line to Jingu-Marutamachi)

Atlantis   BAR

22 🚇 MAP P54, H4

This is a slick Ponto-chō bar that welcomes foreigners and draws a fair smattering of Kyoto's beautiful people. In summer you can sit outside on a platform looking over the Kamo-gawa (terrace closes at 11pm). It's often crowded so you may have to wait a bit to get in, especially if you want to sit outside. (アトランティス; ☎075-241-1621; 161 Matsumoto-chō, Ponto-chō-Shijō-agaru, Nakagyō-ku; cocktails from ¥900; ☻6pm-2am, to 1am Sun; 🚃 Hankyū line to Kawaramachi)

World   CLUB

23 🚇 MAP P54, H4

World is Kyoto's largest club and it naturally hosts some of the biggest events. It has two floors, a dance floor and lockers where you can leave your stuff while you dance the night away. Events include everything from deep soul to reggae and techno to salsa. (ワールド; ☎075-213-4119; www.world-kyoto.com; basement, Imagium Bldg, 97 Shin-chō, Nishikiyamachi, Shijō-agaru, Shimogyō-ku; cover ¥2000-3000; ☻8pm-late; 🚃 Hankyū line to Kawaramachi)

Entertainment

Taku-Taku   LIVE MUSIC

24 ⭐ MAP P54, F5

One of Kyoto's most atmospheric live-music venues, with a long history of hosting some great local and international acts. Check the *Kyoto Visitor's Guide* and flyers in local coffee shops and record stores for details on upcoming events. It can be hard to spot: look for the wooden sign with black kanji on it and go through the gate. (磔礫; ☎075-351-1321; Tominokōji-dōri-Bukkōji, Shimogyō-ku; tickets ¥1500-4000; 🚃Hankyū line to Kawaramachi)

Kamogawa Odori DANCE

25 ⭐ MAP P54, H3

Geisha dances from 1 to 24 May at Ponto-chō Kaburen-jō Theatre in Ponto-chō. (鴨川をどり; ☎075-221-2025; Ponto-chō, Sanjō-sagaru, Nakagyō-ku; seats ¥2300, special seats without/with tea ¥4200/4800; ⏱shows 12.30pm, 2.20pm & 4.10pm; Ⓢ Tōzai line to Kyoto-Shiyakusho-mae)

Shopping

Aritsugu HOMEWARES

26 🔒 MAP P54, G4

While you're in Nishiki Market, have a look at this shop – it has some of the best kitchen knives in the world. Choose your knife – all-rounder, sushi, vegetable – and the staff will show you how to care for it before sharpening and boxing it up. You can also have your name engraved in English or Japanese. Knives start at around ¥10,000. (有次; ☎075-221-1091; 219 Kajiya-chō, Nishikikōji-dōri, Gokomachi nishi-iru, Nakagyō-ku; ⏱9am-5.30pm; 🚃Hankyū line to Kawaramachi)

Zōhiko ARTS & CRAFTS

27 🔒 MAP P54, G1

Zōhiko is the best place in Kyoto to buy one of Japan's most beguiling art-and-craft forms: lacquerware.

If you aren't familiar with just how beautiful these products can be, you owe it to yourself to make the pilgrimage to Zōhiko. You'll find a great selection of cups, bowls, trays and various kinds of boxes. (象彦; ☎075-229-6625; www. zohiko.co.jp; 719-1 Yohojimae-chō, Teramachi-dōri, Nijō-agaru, Nakagyō-ku; ⏱10am-6pm; Ⓢ Tōzai line to Kyoto-Shiyakusho-mae)

Takashimaya DEPARTMENT STORE

28 🔒 MAP P54, H4

The grande dame of Kyoto department stores, Takashimaya is almost a tourist attraction in its own right, from the mind-boggling riches of the basement food floor to the wonderful selection of lacquerware and ceramics on the 6th. Check out the kimono

Traditional lacquerware

display on the 5th floor. (高島屋; 📞075-221-8811; Shijō-Kawaramachi Kado, Shimogyō-ku; 🕐10am-8pm; 🚃Hankyū line to Kawaramachi)

Ippōdō Tea
TEA

29 🔒 MAP P54, G1

This old-style tea shop sells some of the best Japanese tea in Kyoto, and you'll be given an English leaflet with prices and descriptions. Its *matcha* makes an excellent and lightweight souvenir. Ippōdō is north of the city hall, on Teramachi-dōri. It has an adjoining teahouse, Kaboku Tearoom (p53); last order 5.30pm. (一保堂茶舗; 📞075-211-3421; www.ippodo-tea.co.jp; Teramachi-dōri, Nijō, Nakagyō-ku; 🕐9am-6pm; Ⓢ Tōzai line to Kyoto-Shiyakusho-mae)

Wagami no Mise
ARTS & CRAFTS

30 🔒 MAP P54, F5

This place sells a fabulous variety of *washi* (Japanese handmade paper) at reasonable prices and is a great spot to pick up a gift or souvenir. Look for the Morita

Stock Up at the Supermarket

The **Meidi-ya** (明治屋; Map p54, H3; 📞075-221-7661; Sanjō-dōri, Kawaramachi higashi-iru, Nakagyō-ku; 🕐10am-9pm; 🚃Keihan line to Sanjō) gourmet supermarket on Sanjō-dōri has a good selection of imported food and an excellent selection of wine.

Japanese Paper Company sign on the wall out the front. (倭紙の店; 📞075-341-1419; 1st fl, Kajinoha Bldg, 298 Ōgisakaya-chō, Higashinotōin-dōri, Bukkōji-agaru, Shimogyō-ku; 🕐9.30am-5.30pm Mon-Fri, to 4.30pm Sat; Ⓢ Karasuma line to Shijō)

Tokyu Hands
DEPARTMENT STORE

31 🔒 MAP P54, E4

While the Kyoto branch of Tokyu Hands doesn't have the selection of bigger branches in places like Tokyo, it's still well worth a browse for fans of gadgets and unique homewares. It's a good place for an interesting gift or souvenir, from Hario coffee equipment and lacquerware *bentō* boxes to stationery and cosmetics. (東急ハンズ京都店; 📞075-254-3109; http://kyoto.tokyu-hands.co.jp; Shijō-dōri, Karasuma higashi-iru, Shimogyō-ku; 🕐10am-8.30pm; Ⓢ Karasuma line to Shijō)

Kyūkyo-dō
ARTS & CRAFTS

32 🔒 MAP P54, G2

This old shop in the Teramachi covered arcade sells a selection of incense, *shodō* (calligraphy) goods, tea-ceremony supplies and *washi*. Prices are on the high side but the quality is good. Overall, this is your best one-stop shop for distinctively Japanese souvenirs. (鳩居堂; 📞075-231-0510; www.kyukyodo.co.jp; 520 Shimohonnōjimae-chō, Teramachi-dōri, Aneyakōji-agaru, Nakagyō-ku; 🕐10am-6pm Mon-Sat; Ⓢ Tōzai line to Kyoto-Shiyakusho-mae)

Kimono Shopping in Kyoto

Mimuro (みむろ; Map p54, E6; ☎ 075-344-1220; www.mimuro.net; Matsubara, Nishi-iru, Karasuma-dori, Shimogyō-ku; ⏱ 10am-6.30pm; Ⓢ Karasuma line to Shijō) is a great spot for anyone looking to take home a good-quality kimono or *yukata* (light cotton kimono). The English-speaking staff will go out of their way to help you find what you're looking for out of the huge range of colours and designs spread over five floors. Yukata prices start at ¥5000 and kimonos from ¥35,000.

Harajuku Chicago (Map p54, G3; www.chicago.co.jp; Teramachi-dōri higashi-iru, Nagakyō-ku; ⏱ 11am-8pm) is a large vintage clothing shop in the Teramachi covered arcade that sells a good range of second-hand kimonos on the 2nd.

Kamiji Kakimoto   ARTS & CRAFTS

33 🔒 MAP P54, G1

This is one of the best places to buy *washi* in Kyoto. It's got such unusual items as *washi* computer printer paper and *washi* wallpaper, along with great letter writing and wrapping paper. Look for the hanging white *noren* (curtain) out the front. (紙司柿本; ☎ 075-211-3481; www.kamiji-kakimoto.jp; 54 Tokiwagi-chō, Teramachi-dōri, Nijō-agaru, Nakagyō-ku; ⏱ 10am-5.30pm Mon-Sat; Ⓢ Tōzai line to Kyoto-Shiyakusho-mae)

Maruzen   BOOKS

34 🔒 MAP P54, H3

Occupying two basement floors of the **BAL department store** (バル; www.bal-bldg.com; ⏱ 11am-8pm), this excellent bookshop has a massive range of English-language books across all subjects, plenty of titles on Kyoto and Japan, a great selection of Japanese literature, magazines from around the globe and travel guides. (丸善; basement, BAL, 251 Yamazaki-chō, Kawaramachi-sanjo sagaru, Nakagyō-ku; ⏱ 11am-9pm; Ⓡ Hankyū line to Kawaramachi)

Daimaru   DEPARTMENT STORE

35 🔒 MAP P54, F4

Daimaru has fantastic service, a brilliant selection of goods and a basement food floor that will make you want to move to Kyoto. (大丸; ☎ 075-211-8111; Tachiuri Nishi-machi 79, Shijō-dōri, Takakura nishi-iru, Shimogyō-ku; ⏱ 10am-8pm; Ⓢ Karasuma line to Shijō, Ⓡ Hankyū line to Karasuma)

Explore ◈
Gion & Southern Higashiyama

Southern Higashiyama, at the base of Higashiyama (Eastern Mountains), is Kyoto's richest area for sightseeing. Thick with temples, shrines, museums and traditional shops, it's great to explore on foot, with some pedestrian-only walkways plus parks and expansive temple grounds. It's also home to the Gion entertainment district and some of the city's finest ryokan.

The Short List

∘ **Kiyomizu-dera (p68)** Climbing to the top of the Southern Higashiyama district to visit one of Kyoto's most colourful temples.

∘ **Chion-in (p70)** Letting your soul be soothed by the chanting monks.

∘ **Shōren-in (p77)** Sipping a cup of green tea while admiring the sublime garden.

∘ **Yasaka-jinja (p79)** Clapping your hands to awaken the gods at this shrine near Maruyama-kōen.

∘ **Gion district (p72)** Taking an evening stroll through the world of geisha.

Getting There & Around

🚈 The private Keihan line provides access to Southern Higashiyama. Get off at Gion-Shijō or Shichijō Stations and walk uphill (east).

🚌 Kyoto City buses serve various stops in the district and are a good way to access Kiyomizu-dera.

S The Tōzai subway line's Higashiyama Station offers easy access to the northern end of the district.

Gion & Southern Higashiyama Map on p76

Kiyomizu-dera (p68) CEZARY WOJTKOWSKI/SHUTTERSTOCK ©

Top Sight 📷
Kiyomizu-dera

Kiyomizu-dera is one of the city's most popular temples. Built around a holy spring (kiyomizu means 'pure water'), the temple has attracted pilgrims since the 8th century AD. In addition to halls holding fine Buddhist images, the complex includes a Shintō shrine that is associated with matters of the heart – buy a prayer plaque here to assure success in romance.

⊙ MAP P76, D4

清水寺

www.kiyomizudera.or.jp

1-294 Kiyomizu, Higashiyama-ku

adult/child ¥400/200

🕐 6am-6pm, closing times vary seasonally

🚌 Kyoto City bus 206 to Kiyōmizu-michi or Gojō-zaka, 🚆 Keihan line to Kiyomizu-Gojō

A Kyoto Icon

This ancient temple was first built in 798, but the present buildings are reconstructions dating from 1633. As an affiliate of the Hossō school of Buddhism, which originated in Nara, it has successfully survived the many intrigues of local Kyoto schools of Buddhism through the centuries and is now one of the most famous landmarks of the city (the reason it can get very crowded during spring and autumn).

Hondō

The Hondō (Main Hall), which houses a Jūichimen (11-headed) Kannon figure, features a huge verandah that juts out over the hillside, supported by 139 15m-high wooden pillars. Just below this verandah is Otowa-no-taki spring, where visitors drink the sacred waters believed to bestow health and long life. The main hall is undergoing renovations and may be covered, but is still accessible.

Jishu-jinja

Up to the left of the entrance to the Hondō you will find Jishu-jinja, where visitors try to ensure success in love by closing their eyes and walking about 18m between a pair of 'Love Stones'.

Tainai-meguri

Before you enter the actual temple precincts, visit one of the oddest sights in Japan: the Tainai-meguri. By entering the hall, you are figuratively entering the womb of Daizuigu Bosatsu, a female Bodhisattva who has the power to grant any human wish.

★ Top Tips

o Check out the temple's excellent website for information, plus a how-to guide for praying here.

o During the cherry-blossom season, autumn-foliage season and the summer O-Bon season (Buddhist observance honouring ancestral spirits), Kiyomizu-dera holds evening 'light-ups', when the trees and buildings are illuminated.

✕ Take a Break

o Slurp down the signature udon noodles at Omen Kodai-ji (p81), a 15-minute walk from the temple.

o Rest your legs over a cup of *matcha* (powdered green tea) at the traditional teahouse Kasagi-ya (p82).

Top Sight 📷
Chion-in

A collection of soaring buildings and spacious courtyards, Chion-in serves as the headquarters of the Jōdo, the largest sect of Buddhism in Japan. It's the most popular pilgrimage temple in Kyoto and it's always a hive of religious activity. For visitors with a taste for the grand, this temple is sure to satisfy.

◎ MAP P76, D2

知恩院

www.chion-in.or.jp

400 Rinka-chō, Higashiyama-ku

adult/child ¥500/250, grounds free

🕙 9am-4.30pm, last entry 3.50pm

Ⓢ Tōzai line to Higashiyama

Jōdo Buddhism HQ

Chion-in was established in 1234 on the site where Hōnen, one of the most famous figures in Japanese Buddhism, taught his brand of Buddhism (Jōdo, or Pure Land, Buddhism) and eventually fasted to death. Today it is still the headquarters of the Jōdo school, which was founded by Hōnen.

Impressive Temple Structures

The oldest of the present buildings date from the 17th century. The two-storey **San-mon** temple gate (pictured) is the largest in Japan. The immense **Miei-dō Hall** (Main Hall), which measures 35m wide and 45m long, houses an image of Hōnen and is connected with the **Dai Hōjō** hall by a 'nightingale' floor that squeaks as one walks over it. Miei-dō Hall is under restoration and closed to the public. It's expected to be finished in 2020.

Temple Bell

Chion-in's temple bell was cast in 1633. It is the largest temple bell in Japan. It's up a flight of steps at the southeastern corner of the temple precincts. The bell is rung by the temple's monks 108 times on New Year's Eve each year.

Gardens

Walk around the back of the main hall to see the temple's gardens. On the way, you'll pass a darkened hall with a small statue of Amida Buddha glowing eerily. It's a nice contrast to the splendour of the main hall.

★ Top Tips

○ Like most other popular sights in Kyoto, it's best to head here first thing in the morning or late in the afternoon to avoid the crowds.

○ This is a large temple complex so set aside at least a couple of hours to explore it all.

✕ Take a Break

○ Stroll through Maruyama-kōen and into the Ninen-zaka area to the lovely Kasagi-ya (p82) for tea and a sweet.

○ Book in advance and team your visit with lunch at arguably one of the city's best restaurants, Kikunoi (p81).

Top Sight 📷

Gion

Gion is the famous entertainment and geisha quar-
ter on the eastern bank of the Kamo-gawa. While
Gion's true origins were in teahouses catering to
weary visitors to the nearby Yasaka-jinja shrine, by
the mid-18th century the area was Kyoto's largest
pleasure district. The best way to experience
Gion these days is with an evening stroll around
the atmospheric streets lined with 17th-century
traditional restaurants and teahouses.

⊙ **MAP P76, D3**

祇園周辺

Higashiyama-ku

S Tōzai line to Sanjō,
🚋 Keihan line to
Gion-Shijō

Take a Wander

Start off on the main street, **Hanami-kōji**, which runs north–south and bisects Shijō-dōri. Hanami-kōji does get very crowded with tourists in the evening, trying to get a glimpse of a *geiko* (the Kyoto word for geisha).

If you walk from Shijō-dōri along the northern section of Hanami-kōji and take your third left, you will find yourself on **Shimbashi** (sometimes called Shirakawa Minami-dōri), which is one of Kyoto's most beautiful streets, especially in the evening and during cherry-blossom season.

A bit further north lie **Shinmonzen-dōri** and **Furumonzen-dōri**, running east–west. Wander in either direction along these streets, which are packed with old houses, art galleries and shops specialising in antiques.

Geisha Manners

No doubt spotting geisha or *maiko* (apprentice geisha; pictured) dressed to the hilt on the street in Gion is a wondrous experience, and a photo is a much-coveted souvenir of a visit to Japan. However, please keep in mind that these are young women – many of whom are minors – trying to get to work. In Kyoto the sport of geisha-spotting has gotten out of hand, with tourists sometimes blocking the women's paths in order to get photos. Let them through; *maiko* and geisha are professionals – if you want to get close to them, support their art and go to see them perform.

★ Top Tips

○ Evening is the best time to stroll around Gion, when the lanterns are all lit up and you have the best chance of glimpsing a geisha.

○ Be sure to veer off the main drag, where you'll escape the crowds and see some of the area's impossibly atmospheric backstreets.

✗ Take a Break

○ Dine on *kaiseki* (Japanese haute cuisine) in the heart of the action in a beautiful traditional building at Gion Karyō (p82).

○ Drop in for a civilised drink in the stylish Gion Finlandia Bar (p84).

Kyoto Gion & Southern Higashiyama

Walking Tour 🥾

Southern Higashiyama Highlights

The concentration of sights here can be a little daunting, with so many temples, shrines and museums. This walk takes you through neighbourhoods filled with machiya (traditional Japanese houses) home to teahouses and shops, detours through atmospheric backstreets and into temples before cutting through Maruyama Park and ending with a cup of matcha overlooking a stunning temple garden.

Walk Facts
Start Gojō-zaka bus stop
End Higashiyama Station
Length 5km; four hours

❶ Kiyomizu-dera

From Gojō-zaka bus stop on Higashiōji-dōri, walk up Gojō-zaka slope. Head uphill until you reach the first fork in the road; bear right and continue up Chawan-zaka (Teapot Lane). At the top of the hill, you'll come to Kiyomizu-dera (p68). Before you enter the temple, descend into the Tainai-meguri, the entrance to which is just to the left of the main temple entrance. Next, explore the temple complex of Kiyomizu-dera.

❷ Kasagi-ya

Exit along Kiyōmizu-michi. Continue down the hill and take a right at the four-way intersection down stone-paved steps. This is Ninen-zaka, where you will find tiny little Kasagi-ya (p82), which has been serving tea and Japanese-style sweets for as long as anyone can remember. It's on the left, just below a vending machine and a few doors before Starbucks.

❸ Kōdai-ji

At the end of Ninen-zaka zigzag left then right and continue north to the entrance to Kōdai-ji (p77), a stunning temple with beautiful gardens, on the right up a long flight of stairs.

❹ Maruyama-kōen

After Kōdai-ji continue north to the T-junction; turn right at this junction and then take a quick left. You'll cross the wide pedestrian arcade that leads to Higashi Ōtani cemetery and then descend into Maruyama-kōen (p78). In the centre of the park, you'll see the giant Gion *shidare-zakura*, Kyoto's most famous cherry tree.

❺ Chion-in & Shōren-in

From the park, you can head west into the grounds of Yasaka-jinja. Then return to the park and head north to tour the grounds of the impressive Chion-in (p70). From here it's a quick walk to Shōren-in. From Shōren-in walk down to Sanjō-dōri to Higashiyama Station.

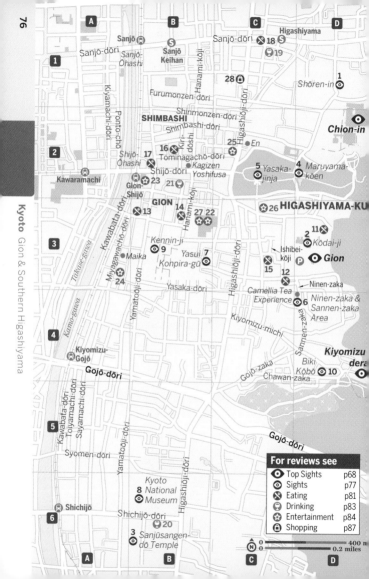

A

Sanjō-dōri

Sanjō-Ōhashi

Kiyamachi-dōri

Ponto-chō

1

2

Kawaramachi

3

Takase-gawa

Kamo-gawa

Kawabata-dōri

4

Kiyomizu-Gojō

Gojō-dōri

5

Kawabata-dōri
Tōyamachi-dōri
Sayamachi-dōri

Syomen-dōri

Shichijō

6

B

Sanjō

Sanjō-dōri

Sanjō
Keihan **S**

Furumonzen-dōri

Shinmonzen-dōri

SHIMBASHI

Shimbashi-dōri

Shijō-
Ōhashi **17 16** Tominagachō-dōri

Shijō-dōri

Gion-
Shijō **23** **21**

GION **14**

13

Kennin-ji **9**

Maika

24

Yasui
Kohpira-gū **7**

Yasaka-dōri

Yamatooji-dōri

Higashiōji-dōri

Hanami-kōji

Kiri-
dōshi

Kagizen
Yoshifusa

28

25 ● En

Higashiōji-dōri

Hanami-kōji

27 22

Gojō-dōri

Yamatooji-dōri

Higashiōji-dōri

Kyoto
National
Museum **8**

Shichijō-dōri

20

3 Sanjūsangen-
dō Temple

C

Higashiyama

Sanjō-dōri **18 S**

19

Shōren-in **1**

Chion-in

5 Yasaka-
jinja **4** Maruyama-
kōen

26 HIGASHIYAMA-KU

2 11
Kōdai-ji

Ishibei-
kōji

15 12 Gion

Ninen-zaka

Camellia Tea
Experience **6** Ninen-zaka &
Sannen-zaka
Area

Kiyomizu-michi

Kiyomizu-
dera

Biki
Kōbō **10**

Chawan-zaka

Gojō-dōri

D

Higashiōji-dōri

Sannen-zaka

Gojō-zaka

For reviews see	
● Top Sights	p68
● Sights	p77
✕ Eating	p81
● Drinking	p83
☆ Entertainment	p84
🔒 Shopping	p87

0 ————— 400 m
0 ————— 0.2 miles

Sights

Shōren-in

BUDDHIST TEMPLE

1  MAP P76, D1

This temple is hard to miss, with its giant camphor trees growing just outside the walls. Fortunately, most tourists march right on past, heading to the area's more famous temples. That's their loss, because this intimate little sanctuary contains a superb landscape garden, which you can enjoy while drinking a cup of green tea (¥500; ask at the reception office, not available in summer). (青蓮院; 69-1 Sanjōbō-chō, Awataguchi, Higashiyama-ku; adult/child ¥500/free; ⊙9am-5pm; S Tōzai line to Higashiyama)

Kōdai-ji

BUDDHIST TEMPLE

2  MAP P76, D3

This exquisite temple was founded in 1605 by Kita-no-Mandokoro in memory of her late husband, Toyotomi Hideyoshi. The extensive grounds include gardens designed by the famed landscape architect Kobori Enshū, and teahouses designed by the renowned master of the tea ceremony Sen no Rikyū. The ticket also allows entry to the small Sho museum across the road from the entrance to Kōdai-ji. (高台寺; ✆075-561-9966; www.kodaiji.com; 526 Shimokawara-chō, Kōdai-ji, Higashiyama-ku; adult/child ¥600/250; ⊙9am-5.30pm; ❑Kyoto City bus 206 to Yasui, S Tōzai line to Higashiyama)

Kyoto Gion & Southern Higashiyama

Gion streetscape

Sanjūsangen-dō Temple

BUDDHIST TEMPLE

3 ◉ MAP P76, B6

This superb temple's name refers to the 33 *sanjūsan* (bays) between the pillars of this long, narrow edifice. The building houses 1001 wooden statues of Kannon (the Buddhist goddess of mercy); the chief image, the 1000-armed Senjū-Kannon, was carved by the celebrated sculptor Tankei in 1254. It is flanked by 500 smaller Kannon images, neatly lined in rows. The visual effect is stunning, making this a must-see in Southern Higashiyama and a good starting point for exploration of the area. (三十三間堂; ☎075-561-0467; 657 Sanjūsangendōma wari-chō, Higashiyama-ku; adult/child ¥600/300; ◷8am-5pm Apr–mid-Nov, 9am-4pm mid-Nov–Mar; ◻Kyoto City bus 206 or 208 to Sanjūsangen-dō-mae, ◻Keihan line to Shichijō)

Maruyama-kōen

PARK

4 ◉ MAP P76, D2

Maruyama-kōen is a favourite of locals and visitors alike. This park is the place to come to escape the bustle of the city centre and amble around gardens, ponds, souvenir shops and restaurants. Peaceful paths meander through the trees, and carp glide through the waters of a small pond in the park's centre. (円山公園; Maruyama-chō, Higashiyama-ku; Ⓢ Tōzai line to Higashiyama)

Lanterns at Yasaka-jinja

Yasaka-jinja

SHINTO SHRINE

5 ⊙ MAP P76, C2

This colourful and spacious shrine is considered the guardian shrine of the Gion entertainment district. It's a bustling place that is well worth a visit while exploring Southern Higashiyama; it can easily be paired with Maruyama-kōen, the park just up the hill. (八坂神社; ☎075-561-6155; www.yasaka-jinja.or.jp; 625 Gion-machi, Kita-gawa, Higashiyama-ku; admission free; ⊙24hr; ⓢTōzai line to Higashiyama)

Ninen-zaka & Sannen-zaka

AREA

6 ⊙ MAP P76, D4

Just downhill from and slightly to the north of Kiyomizu-dera (p68), you will find one of Kyoto's loveliest restored neighbourhoods, the Ninen-zaka–Sannen-zaka area. The name refers to the two main streets of the area: Ninen-zaka and Sannen-zaka, literally 'Two-Year Hill' and 'Three-Year Hill' (the years referring to the ancient imperial years when they were first laid out). These two charming streets are lined with old wooden houses, traditional shops and restaurants. (二年坂・三年坂; Higashiyama-ku; ⓺Kyoto City bus 206 to Kiyomizu-michi or Gojō-zaka; ⓡKeihan line to Kiyomizu-Gojō)

Yasui Konpira-gū

SHINTO SHRINE

7 ⊙ MAP P76, B3

This interesting little Shintō shrine on the edge of Gion contains

Top Tip for Getting Around

This is Kyoto's most popular sightseeing district, so it will be crowded during peak seasons. Walking or taking the train/subway is the way to go as traffic comes to a stand-still and buses are slow and overcrowded.

one of the most peculiar objects we've encountered anywhere in Japan: the **enkiri/enmusubi ishi**. Resembling some kind of shaggy igloo, this is a stone that is thought to bind good relationships tighter and sever bad relationships. (安井金比羅宮; www.yasui-konpiragu.or.jp; 70 Simobenten-chō, Higashiyama-ku; ⊙24hr; ⓺Kyoto City bus 204 to Higashiyama-Yasui)

Kyoto National Museum

MUSEUM

8 ⊙ MAP P76, B6

The Kyoto National Museum is the city's premier art museum and plays host to the highest-level exhibitions in the city. It was founded in 1895 as an imperial repository for art and treasures from local temples and shrines. The **Heisei Chishinkan**, designed by Taniguchi Yoshio and opened in 2014, is a brilliant modern counterpoint to the original red-brick **main hall** building, which was closed and undergoing structural work at the time of research. Check the *Kyoto Visitor's Guide* to see what's on while you're in town. (京都国立博物館; www.kyohaku.go.jp; 527 Chayamachi, Higashiyama-ku; admission varies; ⏰9.30am-5pm, to 8pm Fri & Sat, closed Mon; 🚌Kyoto City bus 206 or 208 to Sanjūsangen-dō-mae, 🚃Keihan line to Shichijō)

Kennin-ji

BUDDHIST TEMPLE

9 📷 MAP P76, B3

Founded in 1202 by the monk Eisai, Kennin-ji is the oldest Zen temple in Kyoto. It is an island of peace and calm on the border of the boisterous Gion nightlife district and it makes a fine counterpoint to the worldly pleasures of that area. The highlight at Kennin-ji is the fine and expansive *kare-sansui* (dry landscape) garden. The painting of the twin dragons

on the roof of the **Hōdō** hall is also fantastic. (建仁寺; www.kenninji.jp; 584 Komatsu-chō, Yamatoōji-dōri, Shijo-sagaru, Higashiyama-ku; ¥500; ⏰10am-5pm Mar-Oct, to 4.30pm Nov-Feb; 🚃Keihan line to Gion-Shijō)

Biki Kōbō

POTTERY

10 📷 MAP P76, D4

Try your hand at making pottery in the Kiyomizu pottery district. This studio is part of the Asahi-dō (p87) complex and offers a few different workshops using electronic and manual pottery wheels. Book ahead. Finished pieces can be shipped to your home at an extra cost. (📞075-531-2181; 1-287 Kiyomizu, Higashiyama-ku; 30-/60-minute workshops

Udon noodles

¥3500/7000; 🕙10am-6pm; 🚌Kyoto City bus 206 to Kiyōmizu-michi or Gojō-zaka, 🚊Keihan line to Kiyomizu-Gojō)

Eating

Kikunoi   KAISEKI ¥¥¥

11 🍴 MAP P76, D3

Michelin-starred chef Mutara serves some of the finest *kaiseki* in the city. Located in a hidden nook near Maruyama-kōen, this restaurant has everything necessary for the full over-the-top *kaiseki* experience, from setting to service to exquisitely executed cuisine, often with a creative twist. Reserve through your hotel at least a month in advance. (菊乃井; 📞075-561-0015; www.kikunoi.jp; 459 Shimokawara-chō, Yasakatoriimae-sagaru, Shimokawara-dōri, Higashiyama-ku; lunch/dinner from ¥10,000/16,000; 🕙noon-1pm & 5-8pm; 🚊Keihan line to Gion-Shijō)

Omen Kodai-ji   NOODLES ¥

12 🍴 MAP P76, C3

Housed in a remodelled Japanese building with a light, airy feeling, this branch of Kyoto's famed Omen noodle chain is the best place to stop while exploring the Southern Higashiyama district. Upstairs has fine views over the area. The signature udon (thick, white wheat noodles) served in broth with a selection of fresh vegetables is delicious. (おめん 高台寺店; 📞075-541-5007; 362 Masuya-chō, Kōdaiji-dōri, Shimokawara higashi-iru,

Kagizen Yoshifusa   🍴

Kagizen Yoshifusa (鍵善良房; Map p76, B2; 📞075-561-1818; www.kagizen.co.jp; 264 Gion machi, Kita-gawa, Higashiyama-ku; kuzukiri ¥1080, tea & sweet ¥880; 🕙9.30am-6pm, closed Mon; 🚊Hankyū line to Kawara-machi, Keihan line to Gion-Shijō) is a Gion institution, and one of Kyoto's oldest and best-known *okashi-ya* (sweet shops). It sells a variety of traditional sweets and has a lovely tearoom out the back where you can sample cold *kuzukiri* (transparent arrowroot noodles) served with a *kuro-mitsu* (sweet black sugar) dipping sauce, or just a nice cup of *matcha* and a sweet.

Higashiyama-ku; noodles from ¥1150; 🕙11am-9pm; 🚌Kyoto City bus 206 to Higashiyama-Yasui)

Chidoritei   SUSHI ¥

13 🍴 MAP P76, B3

Family owned Chidoritei is a snug little sushi restaurant tucked away from the bustle in the backstreets of Gion. It's a great place to try delicious traditional Kyoto *saba-zushi* – mackerel hand-pressed into lightly vinegared rice and wrapped in *konbu* (a type of sea-weed). In summer the speciality here is conger-eel sushi. (千登利

亭; ☎075-561-1907; 203 Rokken-cho,
Donguri-dori, Yamato-oji Nishi-iru, Higashiyama-ku; sushi sets ¥600-2200;
⏰11am-8pm, closed Thu; ☒Keihan
line to Gion-Shijō)

Gion Karyō   KAISEKI ¥¥¥

14 ✖ MAP P76, B3

Take an old Kyoto house, make it
comfortable for modern diners,
serve excellent, reasonably priced
kaiseki and you have Karyō's
recipe for success. The chef
and servers are welcoming and
an English menu makes order-
ing a snap. There are counter
seats where you can watch the
chef working and rooms with
hori-kotatsu (sunken floors) for
groups. (祇園迦陵; ☎075-532-0025;
570-235 Gion-machi, Minamigawa,
Higashiyama-ku; lunch/dinner courses
from ¥5800/11,600; ⏰11.30am-
3.30pm & 6-10.30pm, closed Wed;
☒Keihan line to Gion-Shijō)

Hisago   NOODLES ¥

15 ✖ MAP P76, C3

If you need a quick meal while in
the main Southern Higashiyama
sightseeing district, this simple
noodle and rice restaurant is a
good bet. It's within easy walking
distance of Kiyomizu-dera and
Maruyama-kōen. *Oyako-donburi*
(chicken and egg over rice; ¥1010)
is the speciality of the house.
(ひさご; ☎075-561-2109; 484
Shimokawara-chō, Higashiyama-ku;
dishes from ¥630; ⏰11.30am-7.30pm,
closed Mon; ☒Kyoto City bus 206 to
Higashiyama-Yasui)

Kasagi-ya   TEAHOUSE ¥

(see 6 ◎ Map p76, D4) near Kiyomizu-
dera, you can enjoy a nice cup of
matcha and a variety of sweets.
This old wooden shop has atmosphere to boot and friendly staff
– which makes it worth the wait if
there's a queue. It's hard to spot;
it's a few doors up from Starbucks
up the stairs on the same side.
(かさぎ屋; ☎075-561-9562; 349
Masuya-chō, Kōdai-ji, Higashiyama-ku;
tea & sweet from ¥650; ⏰11am-6pm,
closed Tue; ☒Kyoto City bus 206 to
Higashiyama-Yasui)

Gion Yuki   IZAKAYA ¥

16 ✖ MAP P76, B2

Squeeze in at the counter for
front-row seats to watch the chefs
do their thing at this lively *izakaya*
(Japanese pub-eatery). Seafood
is big on the menu, from sashimi
plates and grilled fish to tasty
tempura, and sake is the drink of
choice – no surprise considering
the owner is a sake brewer. Look
for the short hanging red curtains.
(遊亀祇園店; ☎075-525-2666; 111-1
Tominaga-chō, Higashiyama-ku;
dishes ¥380-800; ⏰5-10pm Mon-Fri, to midnight Sat; ☒Keihan line to Gion-Shijō)

Yagura   NOODLES ¥¥

17 ✖ MAP P76, B2

Across from Minamiza (p84)
theatre, this noodle specialist is an
unassuming and casual spot for a
filling lunch or dinner while exploring Gion. Choose from a range

The Art of the Tea Ceremony

Chanoyu (literally 'water for tea') is usually translated as 'tea ceremony', but it's more like performance art, with each element – from the gestures of the host to the feel of the tea bowl in your hand – carefully designed to articulate an aesthetic experience.

Camellia (茶道体験カメリア; Map p76, D4; ☎075-525-3238; www.tea-kyoto.com; 349 Masuya-chō, Higashiyama-ku; per person ¥2000; 🚌Kyoto City bus 206 to Yasui) is a superb place to try a simple Japanese tea ceremony. It's located in a beautiful old Japanese house just off Ninen-zaka. The host speaks fluent English and explains the ceremony simply and clearly to the group, while managing to perform an elegant ceremony. The price includes a bowl of *matcha* and a sweet.

En (えん; Map p76, C2; ☎080-3782-2706; www.teaceremonyen.com; 272 Matsubara-chō, Higashiyama-ku; per person ¥2500; 🚌Kyoto City bus 206 to Gion or Chionin-mae) is another great little teahouse near Gion where you can experience a Japanese tea ceremony with a minimum of fuss or expense. Check the website for times. English explanations are provided, and reservations recommended. It's a bit tricky to find: it's down a little alley off Higashiōji-dōri – look for the sign south of Tenkaippin Rāmen. Note that it's cash only.

of soba and udon noodle dishes, or opt for the *omakase* – a set of three dishes from the daily specials (¥850). Look for the bowls of noodles on display in the window. (やぐ羅; ☎075-561-1035; Shijō-dōri, Yamatoōji nishi-iru, Higashiyama-ku; dishes ¥950-1600; ⏰11.30am-9pm; 🚌Keihan line to Gion-Shijō)

Bamboo
IZAKAYA ¥¥

18 ✖ MAP P76, C1

Bamboo is one of Kyoto's more approachable *izakaya*. It's on Sanjō-dōri, near the mouth of a traditional, old shopping arcade. You can sit at the counter here and order a variety of typical dishes, watching the chefs do their thing. (晩boo; ☎075-771-5559; Minami gawa, 1st fl, Higashiyama-Sanjō higashi-iru, Higashiyama-ku; dishes from ¥500; ⏰5.30pm-midnight; Ⓢ Tōzai line to Higashiyama)

Drinking

Beer Komachi
CRAFT BEER

19 🍺 MAP P76, C1

Located in the Furokawa-chō covered shopping arcade close to Higashiyama Station, this tiny casual bar is dedicated to promoting Japanese craft beer. There are usually seven Japanese beers on tap, which rotate on an almost daily basis. There's a great bar-food menu and a list of sake if you're not much of a beer drinker.

(ビア小町; ☎075-746-6152; www.
beerkomachi.com; 444 Hachiken-chō,
Higashiyama-ku; ⏱5-11pm, 3-11pm
Sat & Sun, closed Tue; 🛜; Ⓢ Tōzai
line to Higashiyama)

Tōzan Bar

BAR

20 🚇 MAP P76, B6

Even if you're not spending the
night at the Hyatt Regency, drop
by the cool and cosy underground
bar for a tipple or two. Kitted out
by renowned design firm Super
Potato, the dimly lit atmospheric
space features interesting touch-
es, such as old locks, wooden
beams, an antique-book library
space and a wall feature made
from traditional wooden sweet
moulds. (☎075-541-3201; www.ky
oto.regency.hyatt.com; Hyatt Regency
Kyoto, 644-2 Sanjūsangendō-mawari,
Higashiyama-ku; ⏱5pm-midnight;
🚆Keihan line to Shichijō)

Gion Finlandia Bar

BAR

21 🚇 MAP P76, B2

This stylish, minimalist Gion bar in
an old geisha house is a great place
for a quiet civilised drink. There's
no menu, so just prop up at the
bar and let the bow-tied bartender
know what you like, whether it's an
expertly crafted cocktail or a high-
end Japanese single malt. Friday
and Saturday nights can get busy,
so you may have to queue. (ぎをん
フィンランディアバー; ☎075-541-
3482; www.finlandiabar.com; 570-123
Gion-machi, Minamigawa, Higashiyama-
ku; cover ¥500; ⏱6pm-3am; 🚆Keihan
line to Gion-Shijō)

Entertainment

Miyako Odori

DANCE

22 ⭐ MAP P76, B3

This 45-minute dance is a wonderful geisha performance. It's a real
stunner and the colourful images
are mesmerising. It's held throughout April, usually at Gion Kōbu
Kaburen-jō Theatre. The building
is under ongoing renovations until
around 2021 and performances
will be held at Minamiza in the
meantime. (都をどり; ☎075-541-
3391; www.miyako-odori.jp; Gion Kōbu
Kaburen-jō Theatre, 570-2 Gion-machi,
Minamigawa, Higashiyama-ku; tickets
from ¥4000; ⏱shows 12.30pm,
2.20pm & 4.10pm; 🚌Kyoto City
bus 206 to Gion, 🚆Keihan line to
Gion-Shijō)

Minamiza

THEATRE

23 ⭐ MAP P76, B2

This theatre in Gion is the oldest
kabuki theatre in Japan. The major
event of the year is the **Kaomise
festival** in December, which features Japan's finest kabuki actors.
(南座; www.kabukiweb.net; Shijō-
Ōhashi, Higashiyama-ku; 🚆Keihan line
to Gion-Shijō)

Kyō Odori

DANCE

24 ⭐ MAP P76, A3

Put on by the Miyagawa-chō
geisha district, this wonderful
geisha dance is among the most
picturesque performances of the
Kyoto year. It's held from the first
to the third Sunday in April at the

Understanding Geisha

The word geisha literally means 'arts person'. Though geisha are rarer these days, many do still work in Kyoto, in one of the historic geisha districts such as Gion or Ponto-chō. If you're lucky, you might even catch a glimpse of one.

No other aspect of Japanese culture is as misunderstood as the geisha. First – and let's get this out of the way – geisha are not prostitutes. Simply put, geisha are highly skilled entertainers who are paid to facilitate and enliven social occasions in Japan.

Kyoto is the capital of the geisha world. Confusingly, here they are not called geisha; rather, they are called *maiko* or *geiko*. A *maiko* is a girl between the ages of 15 and 20 who is in the process of training to become a fully fledged *geiko* (the Kyoto word for geisha). During this five-year period, she lives in an *okiya* (geisha house) and studies traditional Japanese arts, including dance, singing, tea ceremony and *shamisen* (three-stringed instrument resembling a lute or a banjo). During this time she will start to entertain clients, usually in the company of a *geiko*, who acts like an older sister.

Due to the extensive training she receives, a *maiko* or *geiko* is like a living museum of Japanese traditional culture. In addition to her skills, the kimono she wears and the ornaments in her hair and on her obi (kimono sash) represent the highest achievements in Japanese arts. While young girls may have been sold into this world in times gone by, these days girls make the choice themselves. The proprietor of the *okiya* will meet the girl and her parents to determine if the girl is serious and if her parents are willing to grant her permission to enter the world of the geisha.

It's easy to spot the difference between a *maiko* and a *geiko* – *geiko* wear wigs with minimal ornamentation (usually just a wooden comb), while *maiko* wear their own hair in an elaborate hairstyle with many bright hair ornaments called *kanzashi*. Also, *maiko* wear a decorative long-sleeved kimono, while *geiko* wear a simpler kimono with shorter sleeves.

Miyagawa-chō Kaburen-jō Theatre (宮川町歌舞練場), east of the Kamo-gawa between Shijō-dōri and Gojō-dōri. (京おどり; ☑075-561-1151; Miyagawachō Kaburenjo,

4-306 Miyagawasuji, Higashiyama-ku; with/without tea from ¥2800/2200; ⏰shows 1pm, 2.45pm & 4.30pm; 🚉Keihan line to Gion-Shijō)

Maiko for a Day

If you ever wondered how *you* might look as a *maiko* (apprentice geisha), Kyoto has many organisations in town that offer the chance. **Maika** (舞香; Map p76, A3; ☎075-551-1661; www.maica.tv; 297 Miyagawa suji 4-chōme, Higashiyama-ku; maiko/geisha from ¥6500/8000; 🚉Keihan line to Gion-Shijo or Kiyomizu-Gojo) is in the Gion district. Here you can be dressed up to live out your *maiko* fantasy. Prices begin at ¥6500 for the basic treatment, which includes full make-up and formal kimono. If you don't mind spending some extra yen, it's possible to head out in costume for a stroll through Gion (and be stared at like never before). The process takes about an hour. Call to reserve at least one day in advance.

Gion Odori   DANCE

25 ⭐ MAP P76, C2

This is a quaint and charming geisha dance put on by the geisha of the Gion Higashi geisha district. It's held from 1 to 10 November at the **Gion Kaikan Theatre** (祇園会館), near Yasaka-jinja. (祇園をどり; ☎075-561-0224; Gion, Higashiyama-ku; with/without tea ¥4500/4000; ⏰shows 1.30pm & 4pm; 🚌Kyoto City bus 206 to Gion)

Kyoto Cuisine & Maiko Evening   DANCE

26 ⭐ MAP P76, C3

If you want to witness geisha perform and then actually speak with them, one of the best opportunities is at **Gion Hatanaka** (祇園畑中; www.thehatanaka.co.jp; r per person from ¥22,000; 😊📶; 🚌Kyoto City bus 206 to Higashiyama-Yasui), a Gion ryokan that offers a regularly scheduled evening of elegant Kyoto *kaiseki* (Japanese haute cuisine) and personal entertainment by real Kyoto *geiko* (fully fledged geisha) as well as *maiko* (apprentice geisha). Children under seven years are not permitted. (ぎおん畑中; ☎075-541-5315; www.kyoto-maiko.jp; 505 Gion-machi, Minami-gawa, Higashiyama-ku; per person ¥19,000; ⏰6-8pm Mon, Wed, Fri & Sat; 🚌Kyoto City bus 206 to Gion or Chionin-mae, 🚉Keihan line to Gion-Shijō)

Gion Corner   THEATRE

27 ⭐ MAP P76, B3

Gion Corner presents one-hour shows that include a bit of tea ceremony, koto (Japanese zither) music, ikebana (art of flower arranging), *gagaku* (court music), *kyōgen* (ancient comic plays), *kyōmai* (Kyoto-style dance) and bunraku (classical puppet theatre). It's a hugely touristy affair and fairly pricey for what you get.

Tickets have been discounted from ¥3150 to ¥2500 for foreigners for quite some time. (ギオンコーナー; 📞075-561-1119; www.kyoto-gioncorner.com; Yasaka Kaikan, 570-2 Gion-machi, Minamigawa, Higashiyama-ku; adult/child ¥3150/1900; ⏱performances 6pm & 7pm, Fri-Sun only Dec–mid-Mar; 🚌Kyoto City bus 206 to Gion, 🚇Keihan line to Gion-Shijō)

Shopping

Ichizawa Shinzaburo Hanpu

FASHION & ACCESSORIES

28 🔒 MAP P76, C1

This company has been making its canvas bags for over 110 years and the shop is often crammed with those in the know picking up a skilfully crafted Kyoto product. Originally designed as 'tool' bags for workers to carry sake bottles, milk and ice blocks, the current designs still reflect this idea. Choose from a range of styles and colours. (一澤信三郎帆布; 📞075-541-0436; www.ichizawa.co.jp; 602 Takabatake-chō, Higashiyama-ku; ⏱9am-6pm, closed Tue; 🚇Tōzai line to Higashiyama)

Asahi-dō

CERAMICS

Located in the heart of the Kiyomizu pottery area (see 10 ◎

Minamiza theatre (p84)

Map p76, D4), Asahi-dō has been specialising in Kyōyaki-Kiyomizuyaki (Kyoto-style pottery) since 1870. The complex is called Asahi Touan and comprises the main shop, with the widest collection of Kyoto-style pottery in the city, as well as other shops selling a range of works, including some by the best up-and-coming ceramic artists in Japan. (朝日堂; 📞075-531-2181; www.asahido.co.jp/english; 1-280 Kiyomizu, Higashiyama-ku; ⏱9am-6pm; 🚌Kyoto City bus 206 to Kiyōmizu-michi or Gojō-zaka, 🚇Keihan line to Kiyomizu-Gojō)

Explore ◈
Northern Higashiyama

This area is packed with first-rate attractions and soothing greenery. The main area stretches from Nanzen-ji in the south to Ginkaku-ji in the north, two temples linked by the lovely Path of Philosophy (Tetsugaku-no-Michi). Other attractions include Hōnen-in, a quiet temple, the superb Eikan-dō temple, and the museums around Okazaki-kōen.

The Short List

○ ***Nanzen-ji (p92)*** Immersing yourself in the wonderful gardens, intimate subtemples and a hidden grotto waiting in the woods.

○ ***Ginkaku-ji (p90)*** Taking the bamboo-lined path to see Kyoto's famed 'Silver Pavilion'.

○ ***Path of Philosophy (Tetsugaku-no-Michi; p98)*** Getting lost in thought on this pretty flower-strewn path.

○ ***Hōnen-in (p105)*** Escaping the crowds and finding yourself at this lovely Buddhist sanctuary.

○ ***Eikan-dō (p98)*** Scaling up the steps to the Tahō-tō pagoda to peer down over the city.

Getting There & Around

⌷ **S** The Tōzai subway line is the best way to access Northern Higashiyama.

🚃 The Keihan line stops at stations on the west side of the district.

🚌 Kyoto City bus 5 traverses the district. Several other City buses stop here as well.

Northern Higashiyama Map on p96

Path of Philosophy (p98) TOOYKRUB/SHUTTERSTOCK ©

Top Sight 📷
Ginkaku-ji

At the northern end of the Path of Philosophy, Kyoto's famed Silver Pavilion (Ginkaku-ji) is an enclosed paradise of ponds, thick moss, classical Japanese architecture and swaying bamboo groves. It is unquestionably one of the most luxurious gardens in the city and belongs near the top of any Kyoto sightseeing itinerary.

◎ MAP P96, F2

銀閣寺

2 Ginkaku-ji-chō, Sakyō-ku

adult/child ¥500/300

🕐 8.30am-5pm Mar-Nov, 9am-4.30pm Dec-Feb

🚌 Kyoto City bus 5 to Ginkakuji-michi stop

From Villa to Temple

In 1482 shogun Ashikaga Yoshimasa constructed a villa at this fine mountainside location, which he used as a genteel retreat from the turmoil of civil war. Although Ginkaku-ji translates as Silver Pavilion, this is simply a nickname to distinguish it from Kinkaku-ji (the Golden Pavilion on the other side of town).

The main hall, which overlooks the pond, was originally covered in black lacquer. After Yoshimasa's death it was converted to a temple. The temple belongs to the Shōkoku-ji sect of the Rinzai school of Zen.

Yoshimasa Effigy

In addition to the Buddha image in the main hall, the Tōgudō (residence of Yoshimasa) houses an effigy of Yoshimasa dressed in monk's garb. It also houses a tea ceremony room, which is thought to be the original that all tea ceremony rooms are based on.

The Gardens

You will find walkways leading through the gardens, which were laid out by painter and garden designer Sōami. The gardens include meticulously raked cones of white sand known as *kōgetsudai*, designed to reflect moonlight and enhance the beauty of the garden at night.

★ **Top Tips**

○ Ginkaku-ji is one of the city's most popular sites. Visit when the crowds are likely to be thin: early on a weekday morning or just before closing.

○ A rainy day is a lovely time to visit: the moss here is superb under a light rain.

✕ **Take a Break**

○ Stop in for a break at Omen (p102) for fantastic noodles in an elegant, traditional Japanese house.

○ Goya (p100) is a 10-minute walk away and is a lovely place for lunch, with its menu of delicious and healthy Okinawan cuisine.

Top Sight
Nanzen-ji

Nanzen-ji, a complex of Zen temples and subtemples tucked against the Higashiyama (Eastern Mountains), is the Platonic form of the Japanese Buddhist temple. It's got it all: a fine little kare-sansui *(dry landscape) garden, soaring main halls, great gardens and an incredibly scenic location.*

◉ MAP P96, F7

南禅寺

www.nanzenji.com

86 Fukuchi-chō, Nanzen-ji, Sakyō-ku

adult/child from ¥300/150, grounds free

🕗 8.40am–5pm Mar–Nov, to 4.30pm Dec–Feb

🚍 Kyoto City bus 5 to Eikandō-michi, Ⓢ Tōzai line to Keage

Rinzai HQ

Nanzen-ji began its life as a retirement villa for Emperor Kameyama. Upon his passing in 1291, it was dedicated as a Zen temple. It operates now as the headquarters of the Rinzai school of Zen.

Highlights

At the entrance to the temple stands the **San-mon gate** (pictued; 1628), its ceiling adorned with Tosa- and Kanō-school murals of birds and angels. Beyond the San-mon is the **Honden** (Main Hall), with a dragon painting on the ceiling.

Beyond the Honden, the **Hōjō** hall contains the Leaping Tiger Garden, a classical *kare-sansui* garden. Sadly, a tape loop in Japanese detracts from the experience of the garden.

After visiting the Honden and the Leaping Tiger Garden, walk under the aqueduct and take a hard left and walk up the hill. Climb the steps to **Kōtoku-an**, a fine subtemple nestled at the base of the mountains. It's free to enter and you will have the place to yourself about half the time.

Despite its popularity Nanzen-ji doesn't feel crowded, even during the autumn-foliage season (November), when the maples turn crimson and stand in beautiful contrast to the moss beneath their boughs.

★ Top Tips

o While you're in the Hōjō, you can enjoy a cup of tea while gazing at a small waterfall (¥500; ask at the reception desk of the Hōjō).

o There are several lovely subtemples that surround the complex, including Nanzen-in (p100), Konchi-in (p100) and Tenju-an (p100), so it's worth exploring the area.

o Perhaps the best part of Nanzen-ji is overlooked by most visitors: Nanzen-ji Oku-no-in (p100), a small shrine hidden in a forested hollow behind the main precinct.

✕ Take a Break

o Grab a drink at the casual Kick Up (p104) bar, across the street from the Westin Miyako.

o Take a short walk from the temple and past Eikan-dō for some lunchtime noodles at Hinode Udon (p103).

Walking Tour

A Philosophical Meander

Northern Higashiyama is home to some of the best sightseeing, with Buddhist temple complexes spread out like a string of pearls along the Path of Philosophy. The path follows a cherry-blossom-lined canal and offers some of the prettiest scenery in Kyoto. Dip in and out of temples as you stroll along, taking time to ponder as did the namesake 20th-century philosopher Nishida Kitarō.

Walk Facts

Start Keage Station

End Ginkaku-ji-Michi bus stop

Length About 6km; four hours

❶ Konchi-in

Start at Keage Station on the Tōzai subway line, walk downhill, cross the pedestrian overpass, head back uphill and go through the tunnel under the old funicular tracks. This leads to a narrow street that winds towards Konchi-in (p100), a lovely subtemple of Nanzen-ji with an excellent garden.

❷ Nanzen-ji

Just past Konchi-in, take a right on the main road and walk up through the gate into Nanzen-ji (p92). Take your time to roam around its expansive grounds and don't miss the classic Zen garden, Leaping Tiger Garden. Check out the main hall and sip a cup of *matcha* (powdered green tea) while admiring the waterfall.

❸ Eikan-dō

Return the way you came and exit the north side of Nanzen-ji, following the road through a gate. You'll soon come to Eikan-dō (p98), a large temple famous for its artworks and interesting architecture. Climb up to the top of the pagoda for stunning views over the city.

❹ Path of Philosophy

At the corner just beyond Eikan-dō, a sign in English and Japanese points up the hill to the Path of Philosophy (Tetsugaku-no-Michi; p98), which is the pedestrian path that heads north along the canal. This is one of the most picturesque spots in the city, particularly in cherry blossom season.

❺ Hōnen-in

It's then a straight shot up the lovely tree-lined canal for about 800m until you reach a small sign in English and Japanese pointing up the hill to Hōnen-in (p105). Follow the sign, take a left at the top of the hill, walk past a small park and you'll see the picturesque thatched gate of Hōnen-in.

❻ Ginkaku-ji

After checking out the temple, exit via the thatched gate and take a quick right downhill. From here, follow the narrow side streets north to Ginkaku-ji (p90), the famed Silver Pavilion. Don't miss the superb raked garden and walking path that leads through tall pine trees up the mountainside.

Hōnen-in

PHUONG D. NGUYEN/SHUTTERSTOCK ©

Kyoto Northern Higashiyama

SAKYŌ-KU

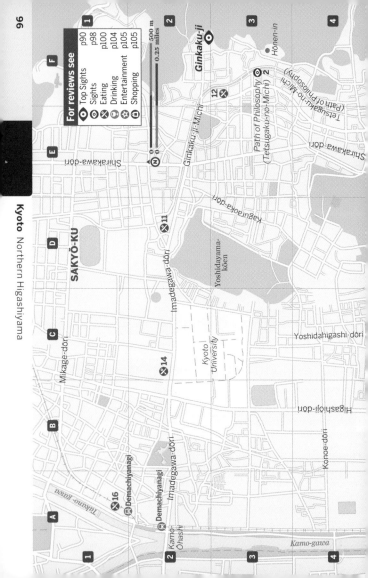

Ginkaku-ji

Hōnen-in

Tetsugaku-no-Michi
(Path of Philosophy)

Path of Philosophy
(Tetsugaku-no-Michi)

Ginkaku-ji-Michi

Shirakawa-dōri

Shirakawa-dōri

Kagura oka-dōri

Yoshidayama-kōen

Imadegawa-dōri

Mikage-dōri

Kyoto
University

Yoshidahigashi-dōri

Higashioji-dōri

Konoe-dōri

Imadegawa-dōri

Demachiyanagi

Demachiyanagi

Kamo-
Ōhashi

Takano-gawa

Kamo-gawa

For reviews see	
◎ Top Sights	p90
◎ Sights	p98
✖ Eating	p100
◐ Drinking	p104
✿ Entertainment	p105
🛍 Shopping	p105

0 ────── 500 m
0 ────── 0.25 miles

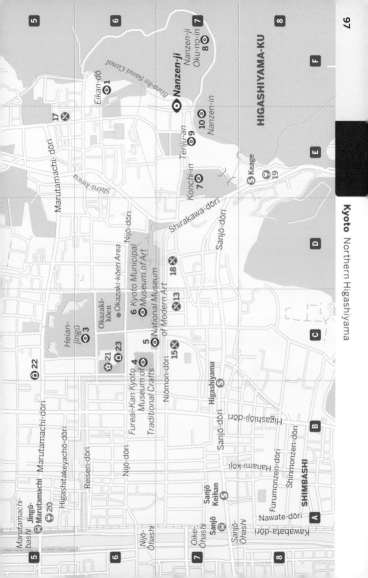

Sights

Eikan-dō
BUDDHIST TEMPLE

1 ⊙ MAP P96, F6

Perhaps Kyoto's most famous (and most crowded) autumn-foliage destination, Eikan-dō is a superb temple just a short walk south of the famous Path of Philosophy. Eikan-dō is made interesting by its varied architecture, its gardens and its works of art. It was founded as Zenrin-ji in 855 by the priest Shinshō, but the name was changed to Eikan-dō in the 11th century to honour the philanthropic priest Eikan. (永観堂; 📞075-761-0007; www.eikando.or.jp; 48 Eikandō-chō, Sakyō-ku; adult/child ¥600/400; ⏰9am-5pm; 🚌Kyoto City bus 5 to Eikandō-michi, Ⓢ Tōzai line to Keage)

Path of Philosophy (Tetsugaku-no-Michi)
AREA

2 ⊙ MAP P96, F3

The Tetsugaku-no-Michi is one of the most pleasant walks in Kyoto. Lined with a great variety of flowering plants, bushes and trees, it is a corridor of colour throughout most of the year. Follow the traffic-free route along a canal lined with cherry trees, which come into spectacular bloom in early April. It only takes 30 minutes to do the walk, which starts at Nyakuōji-bashi, above Eikan-dō, and leads to Ginkaku-ji. (哲学の道; Sakyō-ku; 🚌Kyoto City bus 5 to Eikandō-michi or Ginkakuji-michi, Ⓢ Tōzai line to Keage)

Heian-jingū
SHINTO SHRINE

3 ⊙ MAP P96, C6

One of Kyoto's more popular sights, this shrine was built in 1895 to commemorate the 1100th anniversary of the founding of the city. The shrine buildings are colourful replicas, reduced to a two-thirds scale, of the Imperial Court Palace of the Heian period (794–1185). About 500m in front of the shrine is a massive steel *torii* (entrance gate). Although it appears to be entirely separate, this is actually considered the main entrance to the shrine itself. (平安神宮; 📞075-761-0221; Nishitennō-chō, Okazaki, Sakyō-ku; admission free; ⏰6am-5pm Nov-Feb, to 6pm Mar-Oct;

Getting Around Northern Higashiyama

Many people use Kyoto City bus 5 to access this area – convenient since this bus traverses the entire district – but this bus is often crowded and can be slow. From Kyoto Station or downtown, it's better to take the subway here. Unfortunately, there are no trains or subways convenient to the northern end of this district. A variety of buses will take you to downtown and Kyoto Station. Otherwise, rent a bicycle; this is one of the best ways to explore Northern Higashiyama.

Kyoto City bus 5 to Okazakikoen Bijutsukan/Heianjingu-mae, **S** Tōzai line to Higashiyama)

Fureai-Kan Kyoto Museum of Traditional Crafts

MUSEUM

4 ⊙ MAP P96, C6

Fureai-Kan has excellent exhibits of traditional Kyoto arts and crafts, including woodblock prints, lacquerware, bamboo goods and gold-leaf work, with information panels in English. You can also see a 15-minute *geiko* (geisha) or *maiko* (apprentice geisha) performance, each held one Sunday a month; check the website for details. It's located in the basement of Miyako Messe (Kyoto International Exhibition Hall). The attached shop sells a good range of gifts and souvenirs. (みやこめっせ・京都伝統産業ふれあい館; ☏075-762-2670; www.kmtc.jp; 9-1 Seishōji-chō, Okazaki, Sakyō-ku; admission free; ⊙9am-5pm; **S** Tōzai line to Higashiyama)

National Museum of Modern Art

MUSEUM

5 ⊙ MAP P96, C6

This museum is renowned for its Japanese ceramics and paintings. There is an outstanding permanent collection, which includes many pottery pieces by Kawai Kanjirō. The coffee shop here is a nice place for a break and overlooks a picturesque canal. The museum also hosts regular special exhibitions, so check the website

Raining?

Okazaki-kōen (岡崎公園; Map p96, C6; Okazaki, Sakyō-ku; Kyoto City bus 5 to Okazakikoen Bijutsukan/Heianjingu-mae, **S** Tōzai line to Higashiyama) is an expanse of parks and canals that lies between Niōmon-dōri and Heian-jingū. Two of Kyoto's significant museums can be found here – the National Museum of Modern Art and Kyoto Municipal Museum of Art. If you find yourself in Kyoto on a rainy day, there's enough indoor sightseeing here to keep you occupied.

for what's on. (京都国立近代美術館; ☏075-761-4111; www.momak.go.jp; Enshōji-chō, Okazaki, Sakyō-ku; ¥430; ⊙9.30am-5pm, to 8pm Fri & Sat, closed Mon; Kyoto City bus 5 to Okazakikoen Bijutsukan/Heianjingu-mae, **S** Tōzai line to Higashiyama)

Kyoto Municipal Museum of Art

MUSEUM

6 ⊙ MAP P96, C6

This fine museum holds several major exhibitions a year, as well as a variety of free shows. It's always worth stopping by to see if something is on while you are in town. (京都市美術館; 124 Enshōji-chō, Okazaki, Sakyō-ku; admission varies; ⊙9am-5pm, closed Mon; Kyoto City bus 5 to Okazakikoen Bijutsukan/Heianjingu-mae, **S** Tōzai line to Higashiyama)

Konchi-in

BUDDHIST TEMPLE

7 ⊙ MAP P96, E7

Just southwest of the main pre-cincts of Nanzen-ji (p92), this fine subtemple has a wonderful garden, designed by Kobori Enshū, known as the Crane and Tortoise garden. If you want to find a good example of the *shakkei* (borrowed scenery) technique, look no further. (金地院; 86-12 Fukuchi-chō, Nanzen-ji, Sakyō-ku; adult/child ¥400/200; ⏰8.30am-5pm Mar-Nov, to 4.30pm Dec-Feb; 🚌Kyoto City bus 5 to Eikandō-michi, Ⓢ Tōzai line to Keage)

Nanzen-ji Oku-no-in

BUDDHIST SHRINE

8 ⊙ MAP P96, F7

Perhaps the best part of Nanzen-ji (p92) is overlooked by most visi-tors: Nanzen-ji Oku-no-in, a small shrine hidden in a forested hollow behind the main precinct. It's here that pilgrims pray while standing under the falls, sometimes in the dead of winter.

To get here, walk up to the red-brick aqueduct in front of Nanzen-in. Follow the road that runs parallel to the aqueduct up into the hills, and walk past (or through) Kōtoku-an, a small subtemple on your left. Continue up the steps into the woods until you reach a waterfall in a beauti-ful mountain glen. (南禅寺奥の院; Fukuchi-chō, Nanzen-ji, Sakyō-ku; ad-mission free; ⏰dawn-dusk; 🚌Kyoto City bus 5 to Eikandō-michi, Ⓢ Tōzai line to Keage)

Tenju-an

BUDDHIST TEMPLE

9 ⊙ MAP P96, E7

A subtemple of Nanzen-ji (p92), Tenju-an is located on the south side of San-mon, the main gate of Nanzen-ji. Constructed in 1337, Tenju-an has a splendid garden and a great collection of carp in its pond. (天授庵; 86-8 Fukuchi-chō, Nanzen-ji, Sakyō-ku; adult/child ¥500/300; ⏰9am-5pm Mar–mid-Nov, to 4.30pm mid-Nov–Feb; 🚌Kyoto City bus 5 to Eikandō-michi, Ⓢ Tōzai line to Keage)

Nanzen-in

GARDENS

10 ⊙ MAP P96, E7

This subtemple of Nanzen-ji (p92) is up the steps after you pass under the aqueduct. It has an attractive garden designed around a heart-shaped pond. This garden is best seen in the morning or around noon, when sunlight shines directly into the pond and illuminates the colourful carp. (南禅院; 📞075-771-0365; Fukuchi-chō, Nanzen-ji, Sakyō-ku; adult/child ¥300/150; ⏰8.40am-5pm; 🚌Kyoto City bus 5 to Eikandō-michi, Ⓢ Tōzai line to Keage)

Eating

Goya

OKINAWAN ¥

11 ✕ MAP P96, D2

This Okinawan-style restaurant has tasty food (including vegetar-ian options), a plant-filled stylish interior and comfortable upstairs seating. It's perfect for lunch and just a short walk from Ginkaku-ji.

Temples & Shrines

With over 1600 Buddhist temples and more than 400 Shintō shrines, exploring Kyoto's religious wonders is the work of a lifetime.

Is It a Temple or a Shrine?

The easiest way to tell them apart is to check the gate. The main entrance of a shrine is a *torii* – usually two upright pillars joined at the top by two upright crossbars and often painted bright vermilion. In contrast, the *mon* (main entrance gate) of a temple is constructed of several pillars or casements, joined at the top by a multitiered roof.

Dress Code

Unlike at some other temples around the world, there's no strict dress code as such for temples and shrines in Japan. But it still pays to be respectful. One thing to note is that at most sights you will be required to take off your shoes before entering the temple.

What to Do at a Shrine

If you want to do as the locals do, here is the basic drill: rinse your mouth and hands with pure water at a *temizuya* (small pavilion), using the stone ablution *chōzuya* (basin) and *hishaku* (bamboo ladle) provided for this purpose. Rinse both hands before pouring water into a cupped hand to rinse the mouth. Do not spit the water into the basin; rather, spit it onto the gravel that surrounds the basin. Next, proceed to the *haiden* (worshippers' hall), which stands before the main hall of the shrine. Here, you will find an offering box over which a bell hangs with a long rope attached. Visitors toss a coin into the box, then grab and shake the rope to 'wake the gods', bow twice, clap loudly twice, bow again twice (once deeply, once lightly), and then step back and to the side.

What to Do at a Temple

There are no steadfast rituals you must follow when visiting a Buddhist temple. At many temples, you can pay a small fee for a cup of *matcha* (powdered green tea) and a Japanese sweet, which you can enjoy while looking at the garden.

Choose from simple dishes, such as taco rice and *gōyā champurū* (bitter melon stir-fry), or try the delicious *nasi champurū* – a plate of daily changing dishes. (ゴーヤ;

☎ 075-752-1158; www.goya-asia.com; 114-6 Nishida-chō, Jōdo-ji, Sakyō-ku; dishes from ¥680; ⏱ 11.30am-4pm & 5pm-midnight, closed Wed; 🍴; 🚌 Kyoto City bus 5 to Ginkakuji-michi)

Temple Tips

Visit the big-name sights here – Ginkaku-ji (p90), Eikan-dō (p98) and Nanzen-ji (p92) – early on a weekday morning to avoid the crowds. Alternatively, go right before closing.

Omen   NOODLES ¥

12 🍴 MAP P96, F3

This elegant noodle shop, a five-minute walk from Ginkaku-ji, is named after the signature dish – thick white noodles that are served in broth with a selection of seven fresh vegetables. Choose from hot or cold noodles, and you'll be given a bowl of soup to dip them in and a plate of vegetables (put these into the soup along with the sesame seeds). (おめん; 📞 075-771-8994; www.omen.co.jp; 74 Jōdo-ji Ishibashi-chō, Sakyō-ku; noodles from ¥1150; 🕐 11am-9pm; 🚌 Kyoto City bus 5 to Ginkakuji-michi)

Usagi no Ippo   JAPANESE ¥

13 🍴 MAP P96, C7

Perfectly located for a break when museum-hopping in the Okazaki-kōen area, this delightful restaurant is set in an old *machiya* (traditional Japanese town house) with tatami-mat floors, a small pleasant garden and a cute rabbit theme. The delicious *obanzai* (home-style cooking) sets are great value and might include tasty dishes such as chicken tenderloin wrapped

in *shiso* (Japanese basil). (卯サギの一歩; 📞 075-201-6497; 91-23 Okazaki Enshōji-chō, Sakyō-ku; meals from ¥1400; 🕐 11am-5pm, closed Wed; 🚇 Tōzai line to Higashiyama)

Sujata   VEGETARIAN ¥

14 🍴 MAP P96, C2

Opposite Kyoto University, this humble cafe is a godsend for vegetarians. The menu is limited but the food is fresh, tasty, mostly organic and nutritious, including Indian curries and a Japanese set. There's a few counter seats and tables downstairs and tatami-mat seating upstairs. Sip on authentic homemade chai and relax to the soothing background music. Ask about the free meditation classes. (スジャータ; 📞 075-721-0789; www.sujata-cafe.com; 96-2 Tanaka Monzen-chō, Sakyō-ku; meals from ¥850; 🕐 noon-4pm & 5-7.30pm Mon & Thu-Sat, closes 6pm Sun; 🍴 🚌 Kyoto City bus 206 to Hyakumanben)

Au Temps Perdu   FRENCH ¥

15 🍴 MAP P96, C7

Overlooking the Shirakawa Canal, just across the street from the National Museum of Modern Art, this tiny French-style cafe is a lovely spot to take a break when sightseeing in the area. Check out the delicious cakes on display and pair them with a pot of tea, or spring for a light lunch along the lines of quiche and salad. (オ・タン・ペルデュ; 📞 075-762-1299; 64 Enshōji-chō, Okazaki, Sakyō-ku; tea & cake ses from ¥1100; 🕐 11am-8.30pm Tue-Sun; 🚇 Tōzai line to Higashiyama)

Falafel Garden

ISRAELI ¥

16 ⊗ MAP P96, A1

If you're in need of a break from Japanese food, head to this casual spot near Demachiyanagi Station for excellent and filling felafel pita sandwiches and plates with generous dollops of homemade hummus, or a side of green chilli sauce for more of a kick. There's a small garden courtyard for sunny days. (ファラフェルガーデン; ☎075-712-1856; www.falafelgarden.com; 15-2 Kamiyanagi-chō, Tanaka, Sakyō-ku; felafel from ¥450; ⊙11am-10pm; ✈; ⊠Keihan line to Demachiyanagi)

Hinode Udon

NOODLES ¥

17 ⊗ MAP P96, E5

Filling noodle and rice dishes are served at this pleasant shop with an English menu – the *nabeyaki udon* (pot-baked udon in broth) is a great choice. This is a good lunch spot when temple-hopping in the Northern Higashiyama area. It's popular so you'll probably have to queue. Cash only. (日の出うどん; ☎075-751-9251; 36 Kitanobō-chō, Nanzenji, Sakyō-ku; noodles from ¥750; ⊙11am-3pm Tue-Sat; ⊠Kyoto City bus 5 to Eikandō-michi)

Hyōtei

KAISEKI ¥¥¥

18 ⊗ MAP P96, D7

The Hyōtei is considered one of Kyoto's oldest and most picturesque traditional restaurants. In the main building you can sample exquisite *kaiseki* (Japanese haute cuisein) courses in private tearooms; book months ahead

Gate and canal at Heian-jingū (p98)

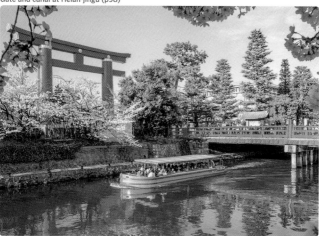

for weekend evenings. If you wish to sample the cuisine on a tighter budget, the annexe building offers *shōkadō bentō* box lunches (¥5400; noon to 4pm Friday to Wednesday). (瓢亭; 📞 075-771-4116; www.hyotei.co.jp/en; 35 Kusagawa-chō, Nanzen-ji, Sakyō-ku; kaiseki lunch/dinner from ¥23,000/27,000; ⏰11am-7.30pm; Ⓢ Tōzai line to Keage)

Drinking

Kick Up   BAR

19 🚇 MAP P96, E8

Located just across the street from the Westin Miyako Kyoto, this wonderful bar attracts a regular crowd of Kyoto expats, local Japanese and guests from the Westin.

It's subdued, relaxing and friendly. (キックアップ; 📞 075-761-5604; 331 Higashikomonoza-chō, Higashiyama-ku; ⏰7pm-midnight, closed Wed; Ⓢ Tōzai line to Keage)

Metro   CLUB

20 🚇 MAP P96, A5

Metro is part disco, part live music venue, and it even hosts the occasional art exhibition. It attracts an eclectic mix of creative types and has a different theme nightly. Metro is inside exit 2 of the Jingū-Marutamachi Station on the Keihan line. (メトロ; 📞 075-752-4765; www.metro.ne.jp; BF Ebisu Bldg, Kawabata-dōri, Marutamachi-sagaru, Sakyō-ku; ⏰8pm-3am; 🚃 Keihan line to Jingū-Marutamachi)

Bridge at Eikan-dō (p98)

Entertainment

ROHM Theatre Kyoto   THEATRE

21 ⭐ MAP P96, C6

Housed in a striking modernist building, ROHM Theatre hosts everything from international ballet and opera performances to comedy shows, classical music concerts and *nō* (stylised dance-drama performed on a bare stage). (京都観世会館; ☑ 075-771-6051; www.rohmtheatrekyoto.jp; 44 Okazaki Enshōji-chō, Sakyō-ku; tickets from ¥3000; ⏰ box office 10am-7pm; Ⓢ Tōzai line to Higashiyama)

Shopping

Kyoto Handicraft Center   ARTS & CRAFTS

22 🔒 MAP P96, C5

Split between two buildings, East and West, this place sells a good range of Japanese arts and crafts, including Hokusai woodblock prints (reproductions from ¥5000), Japanese dolls and a great selection of books on Japanese culture and travel guides. English-speaking staff are on hand and currency exchange is available. Within walking distance of the main Higashiyama sightseeing route. (京都ハンディクラフトセンター; ☑ 075-761-8001; www.kyotohandicraftcenter.com; 17 Entomi-chō, Shōgoin, Sakyō-ku; ⏰ 10am-7pm;

Escape the Crowds

Founded in 1680 to honour the priest Hōnen, **Hōnen-in** (法然院; Map p96, F3; 30 Goshonodan-chō, Shishigatani, Sakyō-ku; admission free; ⏰ 6am-4pm; 🚌 Kyoto City bus 5 to Ginkakuji-michi) is a lovely, secluded temple with carefully raked gardens set back in the woods. The temple buildings include a small gallery where frequent exhibitions featuring local and international artists are held. If you need to escape the crowds that positively plague nearby Ginkaku-ji, come to this serene refuge.

🚌 Kyoto City bus 206 to Kumano-jinja-mae)

Tsutaya Books   BOOKS

23 🔒 MAP P96, C6

Next to the ROHM Theatre, Tsutaya has a small selection of books on Japan, and somewhat pricey bike rental (three hours ¥1500). There's an attached Starbucks, making it a convenient stop when museum-hopping and visiting Heian-jingū (p98) in the Okazaki area. (☑ 075-754-008; 13 Seishōji-chō, Okazaki, Sakyō-ku; ⏰ 8am-10pm; Ⓢ Tōzai line to Higashiyama)

Top Sight 📷
Kinkaku-ji

Kyoto's famed 'Golden Pavilion', Kinkaku-ji is one of the world's most impressive religious monuments. The image of the gold-plated pavilion rising over its reflecting pool is the kind that burns itself into your memory. But there's more to this temple than its shiny main hall. The grounds are spacious and include another pond, a tea arbour and some lovely greenery.

金閣寺

1 Kinkakuji-chō, Kita-ku

adult/child ¥400/300

⏱9am-5pm

🚌Kyoto City bus 205 from Kyoto Station to Kinkakuji-michi, 🚌Kyoto City bus 12 from Sanjō-Keihan to Kinkakuji-michi

A Shogun's Villa

Originally built in 1397 as a retirement villa for shogun Ashikaga Yoshi-mitsu, Kinkaku-ji was converted into a Buddhist temple by his son, in compliance with his wishes. Also known as Rokuon-ji, Kinkaku-ji belongs to the Shōkoku-ji school of Buddhism.

In 1950 a young monk consummated his obsession with the temple by burning it to the ground. The monk's story is fictionalised in Mishima Yukio's 1956 novel *The Temple of the Golden Pavilion*.

The Pavilion & Grounds

The three-storey pavilion is covered in bright gold leaf and features a bronze phoenix on top of the roof. The mirrorlike reflection of the temple in the **Kyō-ko** pond is extremely photogenic, especially when the maples are ablaze in autumn.

In 1955 a full reconstruction was completed, following the original design exactly, but the gold-foil covering was extended to the lower floors.

After visiting the gold-plated pavilion, check out the **Ryūmon-taki** waterfall and **Rigyo-seki** stone, which looks like a carp attempting to swim up the falls. Nearby, there is a small gathering of stone **Jizō figures** onto which people throw coins and make wishes.

Sekka-tei Teahouse

The quaint teahouse **Sekka-tei** embodies the spirit of *wabi-sabi* (rustic simplicity) that defines the Japanese tea-ceremony ethic. It's at the top of the hill shortly before the exit of the temple.

★ **Top Tips**

o Kinkaku-ji is on everyone's 'must-see' list, so it can be crowded. Try to visit early on a weekday morning.

o Another good time to visit is just before closing; the building glows in the sunset and makes for a great photo opportunity.

✗ **Take a Break**

o There are a few eateries on the approach to the temple, as well as a small tea garden near the entrance that serves *matcha* (powdered green tea) and sweets.

o Head to **Gontaro** (権太呂; ☎075-463-1039; www.gontaro.co.jp; 26 Hirano Miyaziki-chō, Kita-ku; meals from ¥850; ⊕11am-9.30pm, closed Wed; ⊡) nearby for tasty noodle dishes and tempura sets in a lovely setting.

★ **Getting There**

🚌 Kyoto City bus 205 from Kyoto Station to Kinkakuji-michi.

Explore ◈
Imperial Palace & Around

This is the greenest area in the city centre; perfect if you're looking to take a break from pounding the pavement. Dominating the area is the expansive grounds of the palace and its park, while to the northwest sits Daitoku-ji – a self-contained world of Zen temples, gardens and lanes. Head north where the greenery continues at the Kyoto Botanical Gardens and the forest setting of the Shimogamo-jinja. This area is also home to Kyoto's traditional textile district, Nishijin.

The Short List

○ **Daitoku-ji (p110)** *Exploring the many temples and admiring the Zen garden at Kōtō-in.*

○ **Sentō Imperial Palace (p116)** *Strolling around the superb gardens here designed by renowned landscape artist Kobori Enshū.*

○ **Shimogamo-jinja (p116)** *Taking a stroll through the long tree-lined approach to this lovely temple.*

○ **Funaoka Onsen (p119)** *Taking a dip outdoors at this iconic old sentō (public bath).*

○ **Kazariya (p119)** *Enjoying a sweet of aburi-mochi (grilled rice cakes coated with soybean flour) and a pot of tea at this 300-year-old establishment.*

Getting There & Around

S Take the Karasuma line to access most of the sights, including the Imperial Palace Park and Daitoku-ji.

🚌 Buses are the most convenient way to visit sights in the far north.

Imperial Palace & Around Map on p114

Kyoto Imperial Palace (p116) LEWIS LIU/SHUTTERSTOCK ©

Top Sight 📷
Daitoku-ji

Daitoku-ji is a separate world within Kyoto – a world of Zen temples, perfectly raked kare-sansui (dry landscape) gardens and wandering lanes. It's one of the most rewarding destinations in this part of the city, particularly for those with an interest in Japanese gardens. Daitoku-ji itself is not usually open to the public but there are several subtemples dotted around the grounds that you can enter.

◎ MAP P114, A2

大徳寺

53 Daitokuji-chō, Murasakino, Kita-ku

🚌 Kyoto City bus 205 or 206 to Daitoku-ji-mae, Ⓢ Karasuma line to Kitaōji

Main Temple

The eponymous Daitoku-ji is the main temple here (on the eastern side of the grounds) and serves as the headquarters for the Rinzai Daitoku-ji school of Zen Buddhism. It was founded in 1319, burnt down in the next century, and rebuilt in the 16th century.

Daisen-in

The two small Zen gardens at popular **Daisen-in** (大仙院; adult/child ¥400/270; ◷9am-5pm Mar-Nov, to 4.30pm Dec-Feb) subtemple are elegant examples of 17th-century *kare-sansui* gardens. Here the trees, rocks and sand are said to represent various spectacles of nature.

Zuihō-in

Subtemple **Zuihō-in** (瑞峯院; adult/child ¥400/300; ◷9am-5pm Mar-Nov, to 4.30pm Dec-Feb) features a rock garden raked into appealing patterns reminiscent of water ripples.

Ōbai-in

Ōbai-in (黄梅院; adult/child ¥600/free; ◷10am-4pm end Mar–early May & early Oct–early Dec) is beautiful in the autumn, when you can see the changing colours. This subtemple is a world of interlinked gardens.

Ryōgen-in

Ryōgen-in (龍源院; adult/child ¥350/200; ◷9am-4.30pm) has two pleasing gardens, one moss and one *kare-sansui*.

Kōtō-in

On the far western edge of the Daitoku-ji complex is the sublime garden of **Kōtō-in** (高桐院; ¥400; ◷9am-4.30pm). It's located within a fine bamboo grove that you traverse via a moss-lined path. Once inside there is a small stroll garden that leads to the centrepiece: a rectangle of moss and maple trees, backed by bamboo. Take some time on the verandah here to soak it all up.

★ Top Tips

○ Try to visit in autumn when the subtemple Ōbai-in is open to the public to see its stunning moss and *kare-sansui* garden.

○ The main gate is on the southeast side of the complex. Pick up an English brochure and map at the information booth here before you start exploring.

○ Kōtō-in is one of the best in all Kyoto. It has been closed for renovations, but should have reopened by the time you read this.

✕ Take a Break

Kazariya (p119) has been grilling its famous *aburi-mochi* sweets for centuries and this lovely traditional teahouse is a great place to enjoy them.

Walking Tour 🥾

Parks, Tradition & Cafe Life

The area around the Imperial Palace Park is where locals escape to when they need a bit of greenery in the city centre. Early morning joggers head to the park, families spend hours strolling through the Kyoto Botanical Gardens and people go about their daily routine at home in their machiya *(traditional Japanese town houses) in the textile district of Nishijin.*

Walk Facts

Start Imperial Palace Park

End Kyoto Botanical Gardens

Length 4km; three hours

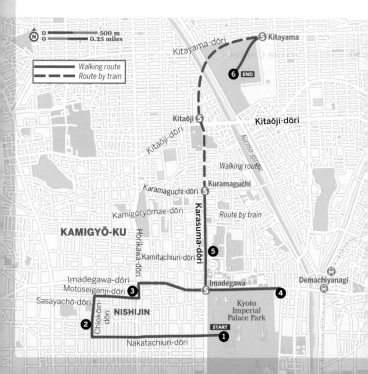

❶ Imperial Palace Park

Rise early and join the locals on a morning jog or brisk walk around the ponds and palaces in the Imperial Palace Park (p116). Stop in to check out the palace itself if you're interested in the Japanese imperial court.

❷ Nishijin

Wander west for a short while and you'll hit the traditional textile district of Nishijin (p117). This can be a lovely place to simply get lost in the backstreets, walking past *machiya* and witnessing the daily life of locals here.

❸ Nishijin Textile Center

While you're exploring the Nishijin area, stop by the Nishijin Textile Center (p119) to get a history lesson on the textile industry in this neighbourhood. You can see artisans at work during a weaving demonstration on the 2nd floor.

❹ Grand Burger

Stop in at Grand Burger (p120), where the locals come to lunch on filling and tasty burger sets that come with crispy fries and coleslaw salad. Make sure you leave enough room for dessert.

❺ Papa Jon's

This inviting cafe (p120) is a favourite of in-the-know locals for delicious cakes and a welcoming atmosphere. Don't miss out on a slice of their excellent New York cheesecake.

❻ Kyoto Botanical Gardens

Catch the Karasuma line to Kitayama station. From here you can access the flower-filled Botanical Gardens (p117) for an afternoon joining local families soaking up the sun; stop in at the greenhouse while you're here.

Nishijin Textile Center

For reviews see

◉	Top Sights	p110
◉	Sights	p116
⊗	Eating	p119
✪	Entertainment	p120
🛍	Shopping	p121

400 m
0.2 miles

KAMIGYŌ-KU

Kitaōji-dōri

Kamo-gawa

Shimogamonaka-dōri

Shimogamo-4 Jinja

Tadasu-no-mori

Shimogamohon-dōri

Kamo-gawa

Izumoji-bashi

Shimogamonishi-dōri

Kamo-kaidō

Kyoto Botanical Gardens

5

Kamigamo Jinja

◉ 6

Kitaōji

Kuramaguchi

Karasuma-dōri

Shimei-dōri

Karamaguchi-dōri

Kamigoryōmae-dōri

Horikawa-dōri

Kitaōji-dōri

Daitoku-ji

⊗ 12

Kenkun-dōri

⊗ 15

Funaoka 9 10 ⊗
Onsen ◉

Kuramaguchi-dōri

Funaoka-higashi-dōri

Teranouchi-dōri

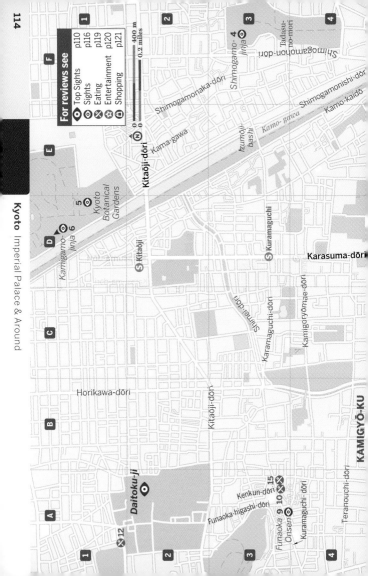

Aoi-bashi

Demachiyanagi

Kamo Ohashi

Kawabata-dōri

Kawaramachi-dōri

Kojinguchi-dōri

Jingū

Marutamachi

Teramachi-dōri

Marutamachi-dōri

14 ✕

Doshisha University

Imperial Household Agency

2 ◎
Sento Imperial Palace

Kyoto Imperial Palace
3 ◎

1 ◎

Kyoto Imperial Palace Park

13 ✕

Imadegawa

11 ✕

Karasuma-dōri

Karasuma-dōri

Shinmachi-dōri

Marutamachi

Nakatachiuri-dōri

Nakachōjamachi-dōri

Kamitachiuri-dōri

Horikawa-dōri

Nishijin
Textile Center
8 ◎

Horikawa-dōri

Inokuma-dōri

16 ✿

Yokoshinmei-dōri

Ichijo-dōri

Motoseiganji-dōri

Kamichōjamachi-dōri

Ōmiya-dōri

Demizu-dōri

Chiokoin-dōri

Jōfukuji-dōri

Uronomon-dōri

Shimotachiuri-dōri

Sawaragichō-dōri

Nishijin
7 ◎

17

NISHIJIN

Imadegawa-dōri

Nakasuji-dōri

Sasayachō-dōri

Senbon-dōri

Sights

Kyoto Imperial Palace Park

PARK

1 🎯 MAP P114, D7

The Kyoto Imperial Palace (Kyoto Gosho) and Sentō Imperial Palace (Sentō Gosho) are surrounded by the spacious Kyoto Imperial Palace Park, which is planted with a huge variety of flowering trees and open fields. It's perfect for picnics, strolls and just about any sport you can think of. Take some time to visit the pond at the park's southern end, which contains gorgeous carp. The park is most beautiful in the plum- and cherry-blossom seasons (late February and late March, respectively). (京都御苑; Kyoto Gyōen, Kamigyō-ku; admission free; 🕐dawn-dusk; 🚇Karasuma line to Marutamachi or Imadegawa)

Sentō Imperial Palace

HISTORIC BUILDING

2 🎯 MAP P114, E7

The Sentō Gosho is the second imperial property located within the Kyoto Imperial Palace Park (the other one is the Kyoto Imperial Palace itself). The structures are not particularly grand, but the gardens, laid out in 1630 by renowned landscape designer Kobori Enshū, are excellent. Admission is by one-hour tour only (in Japanese; English audio guides are free). You must be over 18 years old and bring your passport. Your ticket can be printed or shown on a smartphone.

(仙洞御所, Sentō Gosho; 📞075-211-1215; www.kunaicho.go.jp; Kyoto Gyōen, Kamigyō-ku; admission free; 🕐tours 9.30am, 11am, 1.30pm, 2.30pm & 3.30pm Tue-Sun; 🚇Karasuma line to Marutamachi or Imadegawa)

Kyoto Imperial Palace

HISTORIC BUILDING

3 🎯 MAP P114, D7

The Kyoto Imperial Palace, known as the Gosho in Japanese, is a walled complex that sits in the middle of the Kyoto Imperial Palace Park. While no longer the official residence of the Japanese emperor, it's still a grand edifice, though it doesn't rate highly in comparison with other attractions in Kyoto. Visitors can wander around the marked route in the grounds where English-language signs explain the history of the buildings. Entrance is via the main Seishomon Gate, where you'll be given a map. (京都御所, Kyoto Gosho; 📞075-211-1215; www.kunaicho.go.jp; Kyoto Gyōen, Kamigyō-ku; admission free; 🕐9am-4.30pm Tue-Sun Mar-Sep, to 4pm Oct-Feb, last entry 40min before closing; 🚇Karasuma line to Marutamachi or Imadegawa)

Shimogamo-jinja

SHINTO SHRINE

4 🎯 MAP P114, F3

This shrine, dating from the 8th century, is a Unesco World Heritage Site. It is nestled in the fork of the Kamo-gawa and Takano-gawa, and is approached along a shady path through the lovely Tadasu-no-mori. This wooded area is said to be a place where lies cannot be concealed and is considered a prime location to sort out disputes. The trees here are mostly broadleaf (a rarity in Kyoto) and they are gorgeous in the springtime. (下鴨神社; www. shimogamo-jinja.or.jp; 59 Izumigawa-chō, Shimogamo, Sakyō-ku; admission free; ◷6.30am-5pm; 🚌Kyoto City bus 205 to Shimogamo-jinja-mae, 🚈Keihan line to Demachiyanagi)

Kyoto Botanical Gardens

GARDENS

5 ◉ MAP P114, D1

The gardens occupy 24 hectares and feature over 12,000 plants, flowers and trees. It is pleasant to stroll through the rose, cherry and herb gardens or see the rows of camphor trees and the large tropical greenhouse. This is a good spot for a picnic. It's also the perfect location for a *hanami* (blossom viewing) party, and the blossoms here tend to hold on a little longer than those elsewhere in the city. (京都府立植物園; Shimogamohangi-chō, Sakyō-ku; adult/child gardens ¥200/free, greenhouse ¥200/free; ◷9am-5pm, greenhouse 10am-4pm; 🚇Karasuma line to Kitayama)

Kamigamo-jinja

SHINTO SHRINE

6 ◉ MAP P114, D1

Around 2km north of the Botanical Gardens is one of Japan's oldest shrines, which predates the founding of Kyoto. Established in 679, it is dedicated to Raijin, the god of thunder, and is one of Kyoto's 17

Unesco World Heritage Sites. The present buildings (more than 40 in all), including the impressive Haiden hall, are exact reproductions of the originals, dating from the 17th to 19th centuries. (上賀茂神社; 📞075-781-0011; www. kamigamojinja. jp; 339 Motoyama, Kamigamo, Kita-ku; admission free; ◷6am-5pm; 🚌Kyoto City bus 9 to Kamigamo-misonobashi)

Nishijin

AREA

7 ◉ MAP P114, B5

Nishijin is Kyoto's traditional textile centre, the source of all those dazzling kimono fabrics and obi (kimono sashes). The area is famous for *Nishijin-ori* (Nishijin weaving) and the main attraction is the Nishijin Textile Center (p119). There are quite a few *machiya* in this district, so it can

Kamigamo-jinja

MTAIRA/SHUTTERSTOCK ©

Religion: Shintō and Buddhism

Shintō and Buddhism are the main religions in Japan. For much of history they were intertwined. Only about one-third of Japanese today identify as Buddhist, and the figure for Shintō is just 3%; however most Japanese participate in annual rituals rooted in both, which they see as integral parts of their culture and community ties. New Year's visits to shrines and temples are just one example. Generally in Japan, Shintō is concerned with this life: births and marriages for example are celebrated at shrines. Meanwhile, Buddhism deals with the afterlife: funerals and memorials take place at temples.

Shintō

Shintō, 'the way of the gods', is the indigenous religion of Japan. It locates divinity in the natural world. Its *kami* (gods) inhabit trees, rocks, waterfalls and mountains; however, they can also be summoned through rituals of dance and music into the shrines the Japanese have built for them, where they are beseeched with prayers for a good harvest, fertility and the like. The pantheon of deities includes thousands, from the celebrated sun goddess Amaterasu to the humble hearth *kami*. Shintō has no central scripture, so it is hard to pin down, but one central tenet is purity. Visitors to shrines first wash their hands and mouth at a font (chōzuya) at the gate; many rituals involve fire or water, prized for their cleansing powers. Over time, shrines have accrued specialisations, such as matchmaking.

Buddhism

When Buddhism entered Japan via Korea in the 6th century it didn't so much displace Shintō as envelop it; now there were *kami* and Bodhisattvas (beings who put off entry into nirvana in order to save the rest of us stuck in the corrupt world of time). Several waves of Buddhist teachings arrived on Japanese shores, notably meditative Zen, Shingon (an esoteric sect related to Tantric Buddhism) and Pure Land, which taught of salvation in heaven (the Pure Land). It was the latter that most struck a chord with common Japanese, and Pure Land (called Jōdo-shū) remains the most popular form of Buddhism today. Kannon (the Bodhisattva of mercy and an important Pure Land figure) is the most worshipped deity in Japan.

be a good place simply to wander, particularly around Jofukuji-dōri. Be sure to stop by traditional indigo dye workshop and store

Aizen Kōbō (p121). (西陣; Nishijin, Kamigyō-ku; 🚃 Kyoto City bus 9 or 12 to Horikawa-Imadegawa)

Nishijin Textile Center

MUSEUM

8 🎯 MAP P114, B5

There are displays of completed fabrics and kimonos, as well as weaving demonstrations, plus a shop selling items on the 2nd floor. Unfortunately, it's often overrun by large tour groups. It's on the southwest corner of the Horikawa-dōri and Imadegawa-dōri intersection. (西陣織会館; 📞 075-451-9231; www.nishijinori.jp; Horikawa-dōri, Imadegawa-sagaru, Kamigyō-ku; admission free; 🕐 10am-6pm Mar-Oct, to 5pm Nov-Feb; 🚌 Kyoto City bus 9 or 12 to Horikawa-Imadegawa)

Funaoka Onsen

ONSEN

9 🎯 MAP P114, A3

This old *sentō* on Kuramaguchi-dōri is Kyoto's best. It boasts an outdoor bath, a sauna, a cypress-wood tub, an electric bath, a herbal bath and a few more for good measure. To get here, head west about 400m on Kuramaguchi-dōri from the Kuramaguchi and Horikawa intersection. Look for the large rocks. (船岡温泉; 82-1 Minami-Funaoka-chō-Murasakino, Kita-ku; ¥430; 🕐 3pm-1am Mon-Sat, from 8am Sun; 🚌 Kyoto City bus 206 to Senbon Kuramaguchi)

Eating

Kanei

NOODLES ¥

10 🍴 MAP P114, A3

A small traditional place not far from Funaoka Onsen, Kanei is for soba connoisseurs – the noodles are made by hand and are delicious. The owners don't speak much English, so here's what to order: *zaru-soba* (cold soba; ¥950) or *kake soba* (soba in a broth; ¥1000). Prepare to queue and note that noodles often sell out early. (かね井; 📞 075-441-8283; 11-1 Murasakino Higashifujinomori-chō, Kita-ku; noodles from ¥950; 🕐 11.30am-2.30pm, closed Mon; 🚌 Kyoto City bus 206 to Daitoku-ji-mae)

Toraya Karyō Kyoto Ichijō

CAFE ¥¥

11 🍴 MAP P114, D6

This gorgeous tearoom-cafe is a stone's throw from the west side of the Imperial Palace Park. It's fantastic for a break from sightseeing in this part of town. The menu has some pictures and simple English. (虎屋菓寮 京都一条店; 📞 075-441-3113; 400 Hirohashidono-chō, Ichijō-dōri, Karasuma-nishi-iru, Kamigyō-ku; tea & sweet from ¥1296; 🕐 10am-6pm; Ⓢ Karasuma line to Imadegawa)

Kazariya

SWEETS ¥

12 🍴 MAP P114, A1

There are two restaurants at the eastern entrance to Imamiya-jinja specialising in *aburi-mochi* served with *miso-dare* (sweet-bean paste). Kazariya is on the left side when facing the shrine gate. For over 300 years it has been serving plates of the skewered treats with a pot of tea to enjoy in its traditional teahouse. (かざりや; 📞 075-491-9402; Murasakino Imamiya-chō,

Kita-ku; sweets ¥500; ⏱10am-5pm, closed Wed; 🚌Kyoto City bus 46 to Imamiya-jinja)

Papa Jon's

CAFE ¥

13 🍴 MAP P114, D5

A short walk from the north border of the Imperial Palace Park, this light-filled cafe serves brilliant New York cheesecake (¥550) and hot drinks. Other menu items include breakfast sets, homemade quiche, soup and tasty salads, as well as gluten-free cakes. (パパジョンズカフェ 本店; 📞075-415-2655; 642-4 Shokokuji-chō, Karasuma-dōri, Kamidachiuri higashi-iru, Kamigyō-ku; lunch from ¥850; ⏱10am-9pm; 📶; S Karasuma line to Imadegawa)

Grand Burger

BURGERS ¥

14 🍴 MAP P114, E5

A short walk from the northeast gate of Imperial Palace Park, this burger cafe is a great spot for a break while sightseeing. Prop up at the counter or grab a table and bite into juicy burgers with toppings such as avocado and bacon.

Cherry Blossoms Minus the Crowds

During cherry-blossom season (early April), the city's main tourist sites will be mobbed. If you want to enjoy the blossoms without the crowds, head to the banks of the Kamo-gawa or Takano-gawa, north of Imadegawa-dōri.

Sets come with fries and coleslaw. There's a range of international beers, too. No veg option. (📞075-256-7317; http://grand-burger.com; 107 Shinnyodomae-chō, Teramachi-dōri, Imadegawa-sagaru, Kamigyō-ku; burger sets ¥980-1280; ⏱11am-9pm, closed Tue; 📶; 🚃Keihan line to Demachiyanagi)

Sarasa Nishijin

CAFE ¥

15 🍴 MAP P114, A3

This is one of Kyoto's most interesting cafes – it's built inside an old *sentō* and the original tiles have been preserved. Light meals and coffee are the staples here. Service can be slow, but it's worth a stop for the ambience. Lines out the door are not uncommon. It's near Funaoka Onsen. (さらさ西陣; 📞075-432-5075; 11-1 Murasakino Higashifujinomori-chō, Kita-ku; lunch from ¥840; ⏱noon-11pm, closed irregularly; 📶; 🚌Kyoto City bus 206 to Daitoku-ji-mae)

Entertainment

Jittoku

LIVE MUSIC

16 ⭐ MAP P114, B8

Jittoku is located in an atmospheric old *sakagura* (sake brewery). It plays host to a variety of shows – check *Kansai Scene* to see what's on. It also serves food. (拾得; 📞075-841-1691; 815 Hishiya-chō, Kamigyō-ku; ⏱5.30pm-midnight; S Tōzai line to Nijōjō-mae)

Reservations & Admission to Kyoto's Imperial Properties ⓘ

Visitors no longer have to apply for permission to visit the Kyoto Imperial Palace (p116). The palace, situated inside the Imperial Palace Park, is open to the public from Tuesday to Sunday and you just need to go straight to the main gate for entry. Children are permitted with an accompanying adult.

Permission to visit the Sentō Imperial Palace (p116), **Katsura Rikyū** (桂離宮; http://sankan.kunaicho.go.jp) and **Shūgaku-in Rikyū** (修学院離宮; www.kunaicho.go.jp) is granted by the Kunaichō, the **Imperial Household Agency** (宮内庁京都事務所; Map p114, D6; www.kunaicho.go.jp), which is inside the Imperial Palace Park. You can book tours in advance at the Imperial Household Agency office or by filling out the application form on its website. You must be over 18 years to enter each property. For afternoon tours, it's also possible to buy tickets on the same day at the properties themselves from 11am. Only a certain number of tickets are issued each day, so it's first-come, first-served. Tours run for 60 minutes and you are required to arrive at least 20 minutes beforehand. All tours are free and are in Japanese with English audio guides available. The exception is Katsura Rikyū, which costs ¥1000 and also offers guided tours in English.

Shopping

Aizen Kōbō CLOTHING

17 🔒 MAP P114, B5

In the heart of the Nishijin textile district, in a beautifully restored *machiya*, Aizen Kōbō has been producing its indigo-dyed hand-woven textiles for three generations using the traditional dyeing method known as *aizome*. Products are hand-dyed using natural fermenting indigo and vegetable dye sourced from the Tade plant, native to Japan. (愛染工房; ☎075-441-0355; www.aizenkobo.jp; 215 Yoko Omiya-chō, Nakasuji-dōri, Omiya Nishi-iru, Kamigyō-ku; ⓒ10am-5.30pm, to 4pm Sat & Sun; 🚌Kyoto City bus 9 to Horikawa-Imadegawa)

Nishijin Textile Center FASHION & ACCESSORIES

The Nishijin Textile Center (see 8 ⓞ Map p114, B5) sells a variety of goods fashioned from the textiles for which this part of Kyoto is famous. Goods on offer range from inexpensive change purses and neckties to proper obi. (西陣織会館; ☎075-451-9231; Horikawa-dōri, Imadegawa-sagaru, Kamigyō-ku; ⓒ10am-6pm; 🚌Kyoto City bus 9 to Horikawa-Imadegawa)

Walking Tour 🥾

Arashiyama

*Arashiyama and Sagano is a tourist hot spot
thanks to its knockout scenery and the chance to
escape the city for some nature. That's exactly
why locals and visitors flock here at weekends –
to wander its temples spread out in the hills, stroll
through the bamboo grove, eat at top-rate restaurants and take time out from hectic daily life.*

Walk Facts

Start % Arabica cafe
🚉 Saga Arashiyama Sta-
tion (JR Sagano San-in line
from Kyoto Station)

Finish Kitcho Arashiyama
restaurant

Length About 3km; one
hour

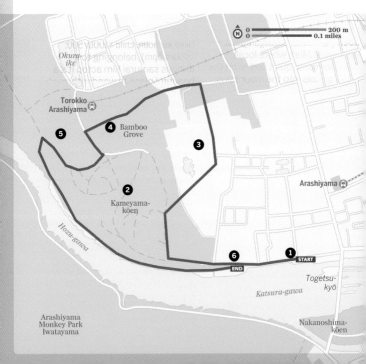

❶ % Arabica

First stop is a good cup of coffee, and **% Arabica** (📞075-748-0057; www.arabica.coffee; 3-47 Susukinobaba-chō, Saga-Tenryūji, Ukyō-ku; ⏰8am-6pm) is *the* place to get it. Baristas serve up expertly made brews at the cafe, which sits in a commanding location opposite the Katsuragawa. Peer through floor-to-ceiling windows looking out to the hills in the background as you order. Grab a takeaway, admire the scenery and take stroll along the river.

❷ Kameyama-kōen

After your caffeine hit, head upriver into the peaceful **Kameyama-kōen** (亀山公園; Sagaogurayama, Ukyō-ku; ⏰24hr), where locals come for some quiet and to hit the walking trails into the mountains. It's also a pretty spot to simply sit and relax with a good book. Occasionally monkeys spend time in the park looking for fruit from the trees, so keep your eyes peeled.

❸ Shigetsu

Once you've had your fill of relaxing in the park, it's time to fill up on lunch. **Shigetsu** (篩月; 📞075-882-9725; 68 Susukinobaba-chō, Saga-Tenryūji, Ukyō-ku; lunch sets ¥3500, ¥5500 & ¥7500; ⏰11am-2pm; 🚫📷) is a lovely restaurant in the grounds of Tenryū-ji, Arashiyama's famous temple, and offers delicious and healthy Buddhist vegetarian cuisine, favoured by temple monks for centuries. Take in the garden views as you fuel up for the rest of your wander around the area.

❹ Arashiyama Bamboo Grove

Take the north gate from Tenryū-ji and you'll find yourself at Arashiyama's most well-known spot. It might be a tourist magnet but who can resist the ethereal beauty of the light peeking through the endless swaying bamboo stalks at the famous **bamboo grove** (嵐山竹林; Ogurayama, Saga, Ukyō-ku; admission free; ⏰dawn-dusk)?

❺ Ōkōchi Sansō

As the bamboo grove comes to an end point you'll find the lavish estate **Ōkōchi Sansō** (大河内山荘; 8 Tabuchiyama-chō, Sagaogurayama, Ukyō-ku; adult/child ¥1000/500; ⏰9am-5pm), belonging to a famous samurai film actor. It's a beautiful place to wander through the stunning garden, which leads up to views across to the mountains. There is also a lovely tearoom here.

❻ Kitcho Arashiyama

Walk back through Kameyama-kōen towards the Hozu-gawa and take in the scenery as you stroll the riverside to your dinner destination. One of Kyoto's best *kaseiki* (Japanese haute cuisine) restaurants, **Kitcho Arashiyama** (吉兆嵐山本店; 📞075-881-1101; www.kyoto-kitcho.com; 58 Susukinobaba-chō, Saga-Tenryūji, Ukyō-ku; lunch/dinner from ¥51,840/64,800; ⏰11.30am-3pm & 5-9pm Thu-Tue) serves delicate dishes in a private room with garden views; you'll need to book well in advance.

Explore ◉
Minami

Minami (ミナミ; 'south'), which includes the neighbourhoods Namba, Shinsaibashi, Dōtombori and Amerika-Mura, is the funny man to Kita's straight man. It's here that you'll see the flashy neon signs and vibrant street life that you expect of Osaka. By day, Minami is primarily a shopping district; after dark, restaurants, bars, clubs and theatres take over.

The Short List

o **Dōtombori (p126)** *Getting an eyeful at this famous, canal-side restaurant strip with flashing neon, intense crowds and the smell of grilling street food.*

o **Tako-yaki (p132)** *Finding your favourite version of Osaka's signature snack – octopus dumplings – at one of the city's many stalls, such as Wanaka Honten.*

o **Amerika-Mura (p131)** *Ambling through this colourful warren of streets crammed with streetwear and secondhand shops, cafes, bars and nightclubs.*

o **National Bunraku Theatre (p136)** *Taking in a performance of Japan's mesmerising traditional puppet theatre.*

Getting There & Around

S Namba and Shinsaibashi subway stations, both on the Midō-suji line, are convenient for this area.

Minami Map on p130

Dōtombori (p126) NIKADA/GETTY IMAGES ©

Top Sight 📷
Dōtombori

Highly photogenic Dōtombori is the city's liveliest night spot. Its name comes from the 400-year-old canal Dōtombori-gawa, now lined with walkways and a riot of illuminated billboards glittering off its waters. Just south and parallel to the canal is a pedestrianised street, where dozens of restaurants and theatres vie for attention with the flashiest of signage.

◎ **MAP P130, C3**

道頓堀

www.dotonbori.or.jp

S Midō-suji line to Namba, exit 14

Glico Running Man

Of all the illuminated signs along the canal, the one for Osaka-based confectioner Glico – a runner triumphantly crossing a finish line – is the most iconic. It first went up in 1935; the sign was last redone in 2014 and is now lit with low-energy LEDs instead of neon. The best view of the sign is from **Ebisu-bashi** (戎橋).

Kuidaore Tarō

Kuidaore Tarō, a drum-banging clown, is another Osaka icon, who represents the city's culture of *kuidaore* (eat 'till you drop). He made his first appearance in the 1950s. The most famous statue of him is at the entrance to the **Nakaza Cuidaore Building** (中座くいだおれビル; 1-7-21 Dōtombori, Chūō-ku).

Kani Dōraku Honten

Dōtombori is full of eye-catching (and literal) shop signs – none more so than the giant animated crab that marks the entrance to **Kani Dōraku Honten** (かに道楽本店; 1-6-18 Dōtombori, Chūō-ku), which is, of course, a crab restaurant. Out front, the shop sells tasty crab sushi rolls (from ¥1200) to go.

Street Food

Dōtombori's pedestrian strip is lined with food vendors fronted by larger-than-life signs advertising *gyōza* (dumplings), *tako-yaki* and more. Two of the most popular pit stops are Kinryū Ramen (pictured; p133), a noodle shop marked by a massive dragon (*ryū* means dragon), and **Daruma** (だるま 道頓堀店; ☎06-6213-8101; 1-6-4 Dōtombori, Chūō-ku; skewers ¥120-230; ⏱11.30am-10.30pm), which specialises in the deep-fried skewers called *kushikatsu* (look for the statue of the angry man holding skewers).

★ Top Tips

○ Signs are illuminated from 6pm to midnight, making this the most popular time to visit.

○ The main strip often gets very, very crowded in the evening, no matter what day of the week it is. The Tombori River Walk, the promenades on either side of the canal, are usually less hectic.

○ Famous food vendors can draw long lines; waits are usually shorter during the day (there are also plenty of non-famous places too).

○ There are some benches for sitting and eating takeaway.

✖ Take a Break

○ If you need a quiet place to sit and eat, duck into noodle shop Imai Honten (p133).

○ Take a coffee break at Jun-kissa American (p136) on the Sennichi-mae *shōtengai* (market street), which runs perpendicular to Dōtombori's pedestrian street.

Walking Tour 🥾

Minami's Greatest Hits

This relaxed evening stroll takes you past some of Minami's best sights, along the atmospheric Dōtombori neon-dazzled strip, then escape to a more quiet and traditional side of the city before ending in the hip, youthful enclave of Amerika-Mura, packed with bars and restaurants.

Walk Facts
Start Shinsaibashi Station
End Shinsaibashi Station
Length 2.5km; 2½ hours

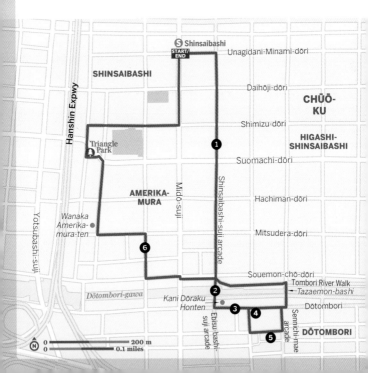

❶ Shinsaibashi-suji

Head out just before dusk to see the daylight fade and the neon lights of Dōtombori take over. Start with a stroll (or shuffle, depending on how crowded it is) down Shinsaibashi-suji (p138), Shinsaibashi's famous, and famously long, covered *shōtengai*.

❷ Ebisu-bashi

Emerging from the arcade, you'll hit the bridge, Ebisu-bashi (p127), the most popular place for photos down the canal Dōtombori-gawa. Among the glowing signs that line the canal, look for the ever-joyful Glico running man.

❸ Dōtombori

Go left past Kani Dōraku Honten (p127), the crab restaurant with the giant animated crab suspended over the entrance – another local landmark. This will take you to the main Dōtombori strip, past restaurants and food stands, marked with evermore outlandish (and literal) signage that takes the plastic food model concept to a whole new level – a giant octopus indicates, for example, a *tako-yaki* stand.

❹ Nakaza Cuidaore Building

On your right look for the drumming mechanical clown Kuidaore Tarō, the mascot for the city's eating culture, at Nakaza Cuidaore Building (p127). Before the big cow, take a right down Sennichimae arcade. Then turn at the cobblestoned alley with the wooden signboard for Hōzen-ji Yokochō.

❺ Hōzen-ji

Now you're suddenly in an older, quieter Osaka, one charmingly lantern-lit in the evening. At the end of the alley, go left then through the temple gateway to tiny Hōzen-ji (p131). Continue past the temple back around to the Dōtombori strip. Cross Tazaemon-bashi and head left on the Tombori River Walk – the promenade that runs alongside the canal.

❻ Amerika-Mura

Cross Shinsaibashi-suji and then turn right, into Amerika-Mura (p131), a fun place to eat and drink in the evenings. Grab some *tako-yaki* to takeaway at the famed Wanaka then head to Triangle Park – the district's popular local gathering spot. From here you can embark on an evening of bar-hopping.

Osaka Minami

A · B · C · D

🍺 15

Hanshin Expwy

Midō-suji

Sakai-suji

🏬 29

Crysta Underground Mall

Nagahori-dōri

Ⓢ Nagahoribashi

Yotsubashi Ⓢ

Shinsaibashi Ⓢ

Unagidani-Kita-dōri

CHŪŌ-KU

SHINMACHI 33 🏬

Unagidani-Minami-dōri

❌ 11

2

NISHI-KU

16 🏬
14

Daihōji-dōri

SHINSAIBASHI

30 🏬

Shimizu-dōri

HIGASHI-
SHINSAIBASHI

Triangle 4
Park ◉

❌
10

🍺 19

Suomachi-dōri

28 🏬

Amerika- ◉ 1
Mura

AMERIKA-
MURA

25 23

Orange St

Hachiman-dōri

Sakai-suji

3

MINAMI-
HORIE

🏬 31

🏬 27

Mitsudera-dōri

Tombori
River
Cruise

Souemon-chō-dōri

18 🍺

Shinsaibashi-suji arcade

6 ◉

Tombori River Walk

Dōtombori-gawa

Tombori River Walk

❌ 12

◉ Ⓓ Dōtombori

24 🏯 Dōtombori

8

21 🏯

9 ❌ 🍺 17

Kamigata Ukiyo-e Museum ◉

5

◉ Hōzen-ji

3   DŌTOMBORI

Ⓢ Nipponbashi

Namba Ⓢ

Namba Ⓢ

Ebisu-bashi-suji Arcade

🏯 Kintetsu
Nipponbashi

4

🚉 JR Namba

Kintetsu
Namba

Midō-suji

35 🏬

13

◉ Kuromon
2 Ichiba

Yotsubashi-suji

NAMBA

Sennichi-mae arcade

Kuromon Ichiba

32 🏬

Namba Nankai-dōri

URA-
NAMBA

❌ 7

🏬 26

5

NANIWA-KU

22
🏯

Midō-suji

Osaka Visitors
Information
Center Namba ℹ️ Ⓢ Nankai
Namba

Nansan-dōri

🏬 34

For reviews see	
◉ Top Sights	p126
◎ Sights	p131
❌ Eating	p132
🍺 Drinking	p135
🏯 Entertainment	p136
🏬 Shopping	p137

6

20 🏯

Nansan-dōri

Ⓝ 0 —————— 400 m
     0 —————— 0.2 miles

A · B · C · D

Sights

Amerika-Mura
AREA

1 MAP P130, B3

West of Midō-suji, Amerika-Mura is a compact enclave of hip, youth-focused and offbeat shops, plus cafes, bars, tattoo and piercing parlours, nightclubs, hair salons and a few discreet love hotels. In the middle is Triangle Park. (アメリカ村, America Village, Ame-Mura; www.americamura.jp; Nishi-Shinsaibashi, Chūō-ku; **S** Midō-suji line to Shinsaibashi, exit 7)

Kuromon Ichiba
MARKET

2 MAP P130, D4

An Osaka landmark for over a century, this 600m-long market is in equal parts a functioning market and a tourist attraction. Vendors selling fresh fish, meat, produce and pickles attract chefs and local home cooks; shops offering takeaway sushi or with grills set up (to cook the steaks, oysters, giant prawns etc that they sell) cater to visitors – making the market excellent for grazing and photo ops. (黒門市場, Kuromon Market; www.kuromon.com; Nipponbashi, Chūō-ku; ☺ most shops 9am-6pm; **S** Sakai-suji line to Nipponbashi, exit 10)

Hōzen-ji
BUDDHIST TEMPLE

3 MAP P130, C4

This tiny temple hidden down a narrow alley houses a statue of Fudō Myō-ō (a deity of esoteric Buddhism) covered in thick moss. It's a favourite of people employed in *mizu-shōbai* ('water trade' – a euphemism for the sexually charged night world), who pause before work to throw some water on the statue. (法善寺; www.houzenji.jp; 1-2-16 Namba, Chūō-ku; **S** Midō-suji line to Namba, exit 14)

Triangle Park
PARK

4 MAP P130, A2

In the middle of Ame-Mura is Triangle Park, an all-concrete 'park' with benches for sitting and watching the fashion parade. Come nighttime, it's a popular gathering spot. (三角公園, Sankaku-kōen; Nishi-Shinsaibashi, Chūō-ku; **S** Midō-suji line to Shinsaibashi, exit 7)

Kamigata Ukiyo-e
MUSEUM

5 MAP P130, B4

This narrow two-storey museum is worth a visit for anyone with an interest in *ukiyo-e* (woodblock prints). It mainly displays prints of famous kabuki actors from the late Edo period. You can also try making your own print on the 3rd floor (¥500, 30 minutes). (📞 06-6211-0303; www.kamigata.jp/kmgt/english; 1-6-4 Namba, Chūō-ku; adult/child ¥500/300; ☺ 11am-6pm, closed Mon; **S** Midō-suji line to Namba, exit 16)

Tombori River Cruise
CRUISE

6 MAP P130, C3

One way to beat the crowds in Dōtombori is to hop on a boat.

Kuromon Ichiba (p131)

Tombori's short, 20-minute trips past the neon signs run on the hour and the half-hour. Night-time is best, though slots fill up quickly; tickets go on sale at the pier an hour before the first cruise of the day starts. Osaka Amazing Pass holders ride free. (とんぼりリバークルーズ; ☏06-6441-0532; www.ipponmatsu.co.jp/cruise/tombori.html; Don Quijote Bldg, 7-13 Sōemon-chō, Chūō-ku; adult/child ¥900/400; ☺1-9pm Mon-Fri, from 11am Sat & Sun; ⓢMidō-suji line to Namba, exit 14)

Eating

Wanaka Honten
STREET FOOD ¥

7 ✗ MAP P130, C5

This famous *tako-yaki* stand, just north of Dōguya-suji arcade, uses custom copper hotplates (instead of cast iron) to make dumplings that are crisper than usual (but still runny inside). There's a picture menu, and tables and chairs in the back. One popular dish to try is *tako-sen* – two dumplings sandwiched between *sembei* (rice crackers). (わなか本店; ☏06-6631-0127; http://takoyaki-wanaka.com; 11-19 Sennichi-mae, Chūō-ku; tako-yaki per 8 from ¥450; ☺10am-11pm Mon-Fri, from 8.30am Sat & Sun; ⓢMidō-suji line to Namba, exit 4)

Chibō
OKONOMIYAKI ¥

8 ✗ MAP P130, C3

One of Osaka's most famous *okonomiyaki* (savoury pancake) restaurants, Chibō almost always has a queue, but it moves fast because there's seating on multiple floors (though you might want to hold out for the coveted tables overlooking Dōtomburi canal). Try the house special *Dōtomburi yaki,* with pork, beef, squid, shrimp and cheese (¥1650). Last orders are an hour before closing. (千房; 📞06-6212-2211; www.chibo.com; 1-5-5 Dōtomburi, Chūō-ku; mains ¥885-1675; ⏰11am-1am Mon-Sat, to midnight Sun; Ⓢ Midō-suji line to Namba, exit 14)

Imai Honten
UDON ¥¥

Located close to Daiki Suisan (see 12 ✖ Map p132, C3) is one of the area's oldest and most-revered udon specialists. Try *kitsune udon* – noodles topped with soup-soaked slices of fried tofu. Look for the traditional exterior and the willow tree outside. (今井本店; 📞06-6211-0319; www.d-imai.com; 1-7-22 Dōtomburi, Chūō-ku; dishes from ¥800; ⏰11am-10pm, closed Wed; Ⓢ Midō-suji line to Namba, exit 14)

Shoubentango-tei
KAISEKI ¥¥¥

9 ✖ MAP P130, C4

That this *kappō-ryōri* (Osaka-style haute cuisine) restaurant isn't more expensive is surprising considering its pedigree: established over 100 years ago, it was a literati hangout in the early 20th century. Even the cheapest course, which includes five dishes decided that day by the chef, tastes – and looks! – like a luxurious treat; reservations are necessary for all but the cheapest course. (正弁丹吾亭; 📞06-6211-3208; 1-7-12 Dōtomburi, Chūō-ku; dinner

Drinking & Dining in Ura-Namba 🍴

Ura-Namba (literally 'behind Namba') is an unofficial district made up of clusters of small restaurants and bars in the shadow of Nankai Namba Station. It's becoming an increasingly cool place to hang out. A good place to start is the Misono Building (p135), a once grand (and now wilting) structure, which has dozens of bars on the 2nd floor.

courses ¥3780-10,800; ⏰5-10pm; Ⓢ Midō-suji line to Namba, exit 14)

Planet 3rd
CAFE ¥

10 ✖ MAP P130, B2

This large, comfortable cafe in Ame-Mura serves good coffee, drinks and eclectic light meals, including pastas, sandwiches, salads and rice bowls. It has trendy decor with big windows for people-watching and a few tablets for guest use. (プラネットサード心斎橋店; 📞06-6282-5277; 1-5-24 Nishi-Shinsaibashi, Chūō-ku; breakfast buffet ¥1080, lunch & dinner mains from ¥880; ⏰7am-midnight; ❄ 📶; Ⓢ Midō-suji line to Shinsaibashi, exit 7)

Kinryū Ramen
RAMEN ¥

Beneath the massive green dragon, this indoor-outdoor spot next door to Daiki Suisan (see 12 ✖ Map p132, C3) offers house-made noodles and a front-row seat to the Dōtomburi scene. Purchase a ticket from a machine, sit at a low table on a tatami platform, top your noodle soup with *kimchi*, garlic or marinated green onion, and slurp away. (金龍ラーメン; 📞06-6211-6202; 1-7-26 Dōtombori, Chūō-ku; regular/chāshū ramen ¥600/900; 🕑24hr; Ⓢ Midō-suji line to Namba, exit 14)

Nishiya
JAPANESE ¥¥

11  MAP P130, C2

A peaceful retreat from the busy streets of Shinsaibashi, this welcoming Osaka landmark serves udon noodles, hearty *nabe* (hot pot) dishes and *shabu-shabu* (thin slices of meat and vegetables cooked in a broth and dipped in sauce) for reasonable prices. Look for the traditional three-storey wooden building with a sliding-door entrance, just north of the corner. (にし家; 📞06-6241-9221; www.nishiya.co.jp; 1-18-18 Higashi-Shinsaibashi, Chūō-ku; dishes & lunch sets ¥650-1700, dinner courses ¥3760-7540; 🕑11am-10pm; Ⓢ Midō-suji line to Shinsaibashi, exit 5 or 6)

Daiki Suisan
SUSHI ¥¥

12  MAP P130, C3

This deceptively big *kaiten-sushi* (conveyor-belt sushi) restaurant has a prime Dōtombori location. Plates are colour coded by price and staff speak some English, too. Non-sushi-eaters can get cooked foods including *tori no karaage* (fried chicken) and fried tuna. (大起水産; 📞06-6214-1055; 1-7-24 Dōtombori, Chūō-ku; dishes ¥100-500; 🕑11am-11pm; Ⓢ Midō-suji line to Namba, exit 14)

Kaiten-sushi restaurant

Drinking

Misono Building
BAR

13 MAP P130, C4

With a waterfall and a grand, spiralling staircase out front, the Misono Building (built c 1956) was once a symbol of the high life. It's now fallen into a kind of decadent decay, making the building a lure for underground culture types, who have turned the 2nd floor into a strip of tiny, eccentric bars. (味園ビル; 2nd fl, Misono Bldg, 2-3-9 Sennichi-mae, Chūō-ku; ⏰6pm-late; S Sakai-suji line to Nipponbashi, exit 5)

Circus
CLUB

14 MAP P130, A2

This small club is the heart of Osaka's underground electronic scene. The dance floor is non-smoking. It's open on Friday and Saturday nights and sometimes during the week. Look up for the small sign in English and bring photo ID. (📞06-6241-3822; www.circus-osaka.com; 2nd fl, 1-8-16 Nishi-Shinsaibashi, Chūō-ku; entry ¥1000-2500; S Midō-suji line to Shinsaibashi, exit 7)

Mel Coffee Roasters
CAFE

15 MAP P130, A1

This tiny takeaway stand – the vintage Probat roaster takes up half of it – raised the bar for coffee in Osaka when it opened in 2016. The owner speaks good English and will happily discuss the taste profiles of the various single-origin hand-pours on offer. (メル・コーヒー・ロースターズ; 📞06-4394-8177; https://melcoffee.stores.jp; 1-20-4 Shinmachi, Nishi-ku; coffee from ¥350; ⏰9am-7pm Tue-Fri, from 11am Sat & Sun; S Yotsubashi line to Yotsubashi, exit 2)

Rock Rock
BAR

16 MAP P130, A2

Serving the music-loving community since 1995, Rock Rock has a history of hosting after-parties for international acts and attracting celeb visitors. Regular events with a modest cover charge (usually ¥1500, including one drink ticket) showcase some of Osaka's finest rock DJs (and famous guests). (ロックロック; www.rockrock.co.jp; 3rd fl, Shinsaibashi Atrium Bldg, 1-8-1 Nishi-Shinsaibashi, Chūō-ku; ⏰7pm-5am Mon-Sat, to 1am Sun; S Midō-suji line to Shinsaibashi, exit 7)

Look Up, Look Down

When wandering the narrow streets of Osaka late at night, convinced that spot you're looking for must have closed or moved, remember that bars and pubs throughout Japan are often tucked away in the upper floors and basements of buildings. Check signs on the sides of buildings showing what's on each floor and learn how to ask 'Where is...?' in Japanese (...wa doko des ka?).

Jun-kissa American

CAFE

17 📍 MAP P130, C4

With its 1940s interior intact and waitresses in long skirts, American is a classic *jun-kissa* – a shop from the first wave of cafes to open in Japan during the post-WWII American occupation. Come before 11am for a 'morning set' (¥620) of pillowy buttered toast, a hard-boiled egg and coffee. Look for the chrome sign out front. (純喫茶アメリカン; 📞06-6211-2100; 1-7-4 Dōtombori, Chūō-ku; ⏰9am-11pm; 🚇Midō-suji line to Namba, exit 15)

Folk Rock Bar Phoebe

BAR

18 📍 MAP P130, A3

Crammed with vinyl and knick-knacks, Phoebe looks like a drinks counter operated out of an old hippie's storage closet (we mean that in a good way). The friendly owner spins folk-rock tunes on the record player, mixes good cocktails and serves tasty food. There's an English-language sign out front. (108 Dōtombori Heights, 2-7-22 Nishi-Shinsaibashi, Chūō-ku; ⏰7pm-2am; 🚇Midō-suji line to Namba, exit 14)

Murphy's

PUB

19 📍 MAP P130, C2

This is one of the oldest Irish-style pubs in Japan, and a good place to rub shoulders with expats and Japanese; enjoy free live music; catch sports matches on TV; dig into pub food such as chip butties and meat pies; and, of course, have a pint (from ¥800). (マーフィーズ; 📞06-6245-3757; www.murphysosaka.com; 2nd & 3rd fl, 1-5-2 Shinsaibashi-suji, Chūō-ku; ⏰5pm-3am Sun & Tue-Thu, to 5am Fri & Sat; 🚇Sakai-suji line to Nagahoribashi, exit 7)

Entertainment

Namba Bears

LIVE MUSIC

20 ⭐ MAP P130, B6

For going on three decades this has been the place to hear underground music live in Osaka. It's a small, bare-concrete, smoky space – well suited to the punk, rock and indie bands that play here. In keeping with the alternative spirit, you can bring in your own beer. Most shows start at 7pm; tickets usually cost ¥2000 to ¥2500. (難波ベアーズ; 📞06-6649-5564; http://namba-bears.main.jp; 3-14-5 Namba-naka, Naniwa-ku; ⏰hours vary; 🚇Midō-suji line to Namba, exit 4)

National Bunraku Theatre

THEATRE

21 ⭐ MAP P130, D4

The classical performing art most associated with Osaka is bunraku, which makes dramatic use of highly sophisticated puppets. Visiting the theatre is a half-day event: shows, which include scenes from different plays, top four hours. Too long? Unreserved, same-day single-act tickets are sold, when available, at the venue from 10am. Rent the English-language audio guide (full performance/single act ¥650/300). (国立文楽

劇場; 📞06-6212-2531, ticket centre 0570-07-9900; www.ntj.jac.go.jp; 1-12-10 Nipponbashi, Chūō-ku; full performances ¥2400-6000, single acts ¥500-1500; ⏰opening months vary, check the website; 🚇Sakai-suji line to Nipponbashi, exit 7)

Sumo Spring Tournament
SPECTATOR SPORT

22 ⭐ MAP P130, B5

The big fellas rumble into Osaka in March for this major tournament, held in the EDION Arena (Osaka Prefectural Gymnasium (府立体育会館) in Namba. Tickets (from ¥3800) go on sale in early February and can be purchased online. (Haru Bashō; www.sumo.or.jp; EDION Arena; ⏰Mar)

Hokage
LIVE MUSIC

23 ⭐ MAP P130, B3

Looking like an office with the inner walls ripped out (which is entirely likely), Hokage seems to be made for its rock, punk and noise bands. It's a small space, where the band might take up half the room, and a good place to discover local bands. (火影; 📞06-6211-2855; www.musicbarhokage.net; basement fl, 2-9-36 Nishi-Shinsaibashi, Chūō-ku; tickets around ¥1500; ⏰hours vary; 🚇Midō-suji line to Shinsaibashi, exit 7)

Osaka Shochiku-za
THEATRE

24 ⭐ MAP P130, B3

This neo-Renaissance building (1923), modelled after Milan's La Scala, was the first Western-style theatre built in Kansai. It occasionally hosts kabuki performances, though unfortunately an earphone guide with simultaneous translation is not available. (大阪松竹座; 📞06-6214-2211; www.kabuki-bito.jp; 1-9-19 Dōtombori, Chūō-ku; ⏰box office 10am-6pm; 🚇Midō-suji line to Namba, exit 14)

Shopping

Time Bomb Records
MUSIC

25 🔒 MAP P130, B3

One of the best record shops in the city, Time Bomb stocks an excellent collection of vinyl and CDs from '60s pop and '70s punk to alternative, soul and psychedelic.

Osaka's Music Scene

Osaka's lack of conservatism and boisterous sensibilities are evident in its underground music scene, which leans heavily towards raucous rock 'n' roll, punk, indie and experimental noise. The city has introduced the world to bands including Shonen Knife and the Boredoms, and it's home to a number of character-filled venues where you can catch up-and-coming and established bands. See what's on at Namba Bears (p136) and Hokage, in Amerika-Mura.

Find out about gigs around town here, too. (📞 06-6213-5079; www.timebomb.co.jp; B1, 9-28 Nishi-Shinsaibashi, Chūō-ku; ⏱ noon-9pm; Ⓢ Midō-suji line to Shinsaibashi, exit 7)

Dōguya-suji Arcade   MARKET

26 📍 MAP P130, C5

This long arcade sells just about anything related to the preparation, consumption and selling of Osaka's principal passion: food. There's everything from bamboo steamers and lacquer miso soup bowls to shopfront lanterns, plastic food models and, of course, moulded hotplates for making *tako-yaki*. Hours vary by store. (道具屋筋; www.doguyasuji.or.jp/map_eng.html; Sennichi-mae, Chūō-ku; ⏱ 10am-6pm; Ⓢ Midō-suji line to Namba, exit 4)

Standard Books   BOOKS

27 📍 MAP P130, B3

This cult-fave Osaka bookshop prides itself on not stocking any bestsellers. Instead, it's stocked with small-press finds, art books, indie comics and the like, plus CDs, quirky fashion items and accessories. (スタンダードブックストア; 📞 06-6484-2239; www.standardbookstore.com; 2-2-12 Nishi-Shinsaibashi, Chūō-ku; ⏱ 11am-10.30pm; Ⓢ Midō-suji line to Shinsaibashi, exit 7)

Flake Records   MUSIC

28 📍 MAP P130, A2

Flake is Osaka's most in-the-know music shop, selling new and used, Japanese and imported, CDs and vinyl. The owner speaks some English; ask him for his recommendations on local bands. This is also a good place to pick up flyers for live music events, and it has listening stations. (📞 06-6534-7411; www.flakerecords.com; No 201, 2nd fl, Sono Yotsubashi Bldg, 1-11-9 Minami-Horie, Nishi-ku; ⏱ noon-9pm; Ⓢ Yotsubashi line to Yotsubashi, exit 6)

Tokyu Hands   DEPARTMENT STORE

29 📍 MAP P130, C1

Nominally a DIY and homewares chain, Tokyu Hands is Japan's favourite place to browse for items you probably didn't need but will end up loving. It's stacked floor-upon-floor with everything from obscure tools to design-forward lighting, clocks, curios and craft supplies, just for starters. There's a smaller branch in Umeda (p154). (東急ハンズ; www.tokyu-hands.co.jp; 3-4-12 Minami-Senba, Chūō-ku; ⏱ 10am-9pm; Ⓢ Midō-suji line to Shinsaibashi, exit 1)

Shinsaibashi-suji Shōtengai   SHOPPING CENTRE

30 📍 MAP P130, B2

East of Midō-suji, Shinsaibashi is one of Japan's great shopping zones, most notably in this eight-block-long covered arcade that's crammed with domestic and international clothing brands, chemists, bookshops and other sundry retailers. On weekends it's estimated that the arcade attracts 100,000-plus shoppers, so expect crowds. (心斎橋筋商店街; www.

shinsaibashi.or.jp; **S** Midō-suji line to Shinsaibashi, exit 4)

Mandarake Shinsaibashi
TOYS, BOOKS

31 🔒 MAP P130, B3

Lose hours browsing four floors of retro Japanese toys (Astroboy!), collectable figurines, manga (Japanese comics), DVDs, art and counterculture books, *cosplay* (costume play) uniforms and more. (まんだらけ; 📞06-6212-0771; http://earth.mandarake.co.jp/shop/gcs; 2-9-22 Nishi-Shinsaibashi, Chūō-ku; ⊕noon-8pm; **S** Midō-suji line to Shinsaibashi, exit 7)

Osaka Takashimaya
DEPARTMENT STORE

32 🔒 MAP P130, B5

This is the flagship of the long-running Osaka-based department store Takashimaya, which stocks mostly international brands, though the homewares selection on the 6th floor is worth a look for local finds. Head to the basement food hall to be tempted by Japanese sweets and bentō (boxed meals). (大阪タカシマヤ; www.takashimaya.co.jp/osaka; 5-1-5 Namba, Chūō-ku; 10am-8pm; **S** Midō-suji line to Namba, exit 4)

Village Vanguard
BOOKS

33 🔒 MAP P130, A2

Village Vanguard bills itself as an 'exciting' bookshop, and it stocks fun, nontraditional, pop- and street-inspired mementos of your time in Japan. Between the cluttered book and magazine racks are offbeat T-shirts and accessories, novelty gifts, homewares and more. (ヴィレッジヴァンガード; www.village-v.co.jp; 1-10-28 Nishi-Shinsaibashi, Chūō-ku; ⊕11am-11pm; **S** Midō-suji line to Shinsaibashi, exit 7)

Namba Parks
MALL

34 🔒 MAP P130, C5

Named for the terraces and trees worked into the open-air layout, Namba Parks features six floors of fashion, accessories, homewares and more, plus numerous restaurants, cafes and a cinema. (なんばパークス; www.nambaparks.com; 2-10-70 Namba-naka, Naniwa-ku; ⊕shops 11am-9pm, dining to 11pm; **S** Midō-suji line to Namba, exit 4)

Bic Camera
ELECTRONICS

35 🔒 MAP P130, C4

This vast shop sells everything related to cameras, electronics and computers at competitive prices. It's a good spot to pick up a travel SIM card, too. (ビックカメラ; www.biccamera.co.jp; 2-10-1 Sennichi-mae, Chūō-ku; ⊕10am-9pm; **S** Midō-suji line to Namba, exit 4)

Top Sight 📷
Osaka-jō

After unifying Japan in the late 16th century, General Toyotomi Hideyoshi built this castle (1583) as a display of power, using, it's said, the labour of 100,000 workers. Although the present structure is a 1931 concrete reconstruction (refurbished in 1997), it's nonetheless quite a sight, looming dramatically over the surrounding park and moat. Inside, a museum displays historical artefacts.

大阪城; Osaka Castle

www.osakacastle.net

1-1 Osaka-jō, Chūō-ku

grounds/castle keep free/¥600, combined with Osaka Museum of History ¥900

🕐9am-5pm, open later at certain times in spring & summer

S Chūō line to Tanimachi 4-chōme, exit 9, **R** JR Loop line to Osaka-jō-kōen

The Castle Walls

Hideyoshi's original granite structure was said to be impregnable, yet it was destroyed in 1614 by the armies of Tokugawa Ieyasu (the founder of the Tokugawa shogunate). Ieyasu had the castle rebuilt – using the latest advancements to create terrifically imposing walls of enormous stones. The largest are estimated to weigh over a 100 tonnes; others are engraved with the crests of feudal lords.

The Turrets & Gates

There are 13 structures on the castle grounds that date back to the 17th-century reconstruction of the castle. **Sengan-yagura** (千貫櫓, Sengan Turret), next to **Ote-mon** (大手門), the main gate, on the western side of the castle, and **Inui-yagura** (乾櫓, Inui Turret), on the northwest corner of the grounds, are the oldest: both date to 1620.

The Main Keep & Museum

By the 20th century, most of the castle was in ruins. Osaka citizens raised money themselves to rebuild the main keep; in 1931 the new tower was revealed, with bright white walls and glittering gold-leaf tigers stalking the eaves. Inside, a museum displays historical artefacts, paintings, scrolls and suits of armour from the feudal era.

You can take an elevator up to the 5th floor of the keep, but you have to hike the rest of the way to the 8th floor (visitors with disabilities can take the elevator to the 8th floor).

The Grounds

From the 8th-floor observatory inside the main keep, there are excellent views of the castle's sprawling, grassy grounds. For local residents, these grounds are the ultimate draw of the historic structure. Where soldiers once trained, families and couples now enjoy picnics and strolls. It's free to walk the castle grounds; admission is for the main keep only.

★ Top Tips

o Return at night to see the castle illuminated by floodlights.

o Visit the grounds on a warm weekend and you might catch local musicians staging casual shows on the lawns.

o The main keep, with its stairs and crowded passageways, can be challenging with small children.

✕ Take a Break

o Vendors gather outside the main gate, selling street food.

o You can pick up gourmet picnic supplies at bakery **Gout** (グウ; ☎06-6585-0833; 1-1-10 Honmachi, Chūō-ku; bread from ¥200; ⏰7.30am-8pm, closed Thu; 🚇).

o Take the Tanimachi subway line one stop to Tanimachi 6-chōme and get a curry lunch at **Kyū-yamu-tei** (旧ヤム邸; ☎06-6762-8619; www.kyuyamutei.web.fc2.com; 6-4-23 Tanimachi, Chūō-ku; lunch/dinner from ¥950/1275; ⏰11.30am-2pm & 6-9.30pm, closed Mon & every 2nd Tue).

Explore ⊚

Kita

Kita (キタ; 'north') is the city's centre of gravity by day in office buildings, department stores and shopping complexes – plus the transit hubs of JR Osaka and Hankyū Umeda Stations (and the multiple train and subway lines converging here). While there are few great attractions here, there is plenty of big-city bustle both on street level and in the extensive network of underground passages below.

The Short List

○ **Umeda Sky Building (p145)** *Taking in the Osaka city skyline views from the observation deck here.*

○ **Yotaro Honten (p146)** *Indulging in delicious tempura at this Michelin-starred restaurant.*

○ **Shopping (p153)** *Giving the credit card a beating at some of the city's best department stores.*

○ **Craft beer (p149)** *Sampling some of Japan's tastiest brews at specialist craft beer bars.*

Getting There & Around

🚇 In Kita you'll find the transit hubs of JR Osaka and Hankyū Umeda Stations (multiple train and subway lines converge here).

Kita Map on p144

Umeda Sky Building (p145)

For reviews see
- ◉ Sights p145
- ✕ Eating p146
- 🍷 Drinking p149
- ★ Entertainment p153
- 🛍 Shopping p153

TOYOSAKI

🍷 14

22

Nakazakichō Ⓢ

400 m
0.2 miles

KITA-KU

1 Umeda Sky
Building

7

24

CHAYAMACHI

20 ★

Miyakojima-dōri

Umekita
Dining

29

Hankyū
Umeda

9

KITA-KU

Underground Passage
to Umeda Sky Building

17

25

DŌYAMA-
CHŌ

18

16

26

Osaka Visitors
Information Center Umeda ℹ

Umeda Ⓢ

21

Hankyū-Higashi Arcade

Eki
Marché

6

JR Osaka

28

Hanshin
Umeda

8

SONEZAKI

Umesan-kōji

Nishi-
Umeda Ⓢ

UMEDA

3 O-hatsu
Ten-jin

10

23

Kissa Madura

Kita-Shinchi

19

27

SHINCHI

KITA-
SHINCHI

Keihan
Watanabebashi

13

Dōjima-gawa

Keihan
Ōebashi

Keihan
Naniwabashi

Museum
of Oriental
Ceramics

2

Tosabori-gawa

NAKA-NO-SHIMA

National
Museum of
Art, Osaka

4

Higobashi Ⓢ

Keihan
Yodoyabashi

12

15

Kitahama Ⓢ

Graf
Studio

11

Yodoyabashi Ⓢ

5

Yotsubashi-suji

Mido-suji

Sakai-suji

SEMBA

Sights

Umeda Sky Building

NOTABLE BUILDING

1 ◉ MAP P144, A2

Osaka's landmark Sky Building (1993) resembles a 40-storey, space-age Arc de Triomphe. Twin towers are connected at the top by a 'floating garden' (really a garden-free observation deck), which was constructed on the ground and then hoisted up. The 360-degree city views from here are breathtaking day or night. Getting there is half the fun – an escalator in a see-through tube takes you up the last five storeys (not for vertigo sufferers). The architect, Hara Hiroshi, also designed Kyoto Station (p40). (梅田スカイビル; ☎06-6440-3855; www.kuchu-teien.com; 1-1-88 Ōyodonaka, Kita-ku; adult/child ¥1500/700; ⏰observation decks 9.30am-10.30pm, last entry 10pm; 🚃JR Osaka, north central exit)

Museum of Oriental Ceramics

MUSEUM

2 ◉ MAP P144, D5

This museum has one of the world's finest collections of Chinese and Korean ceramics, with smaller galleries of Japanese ceramics and Chinese snuff bottles. At any one time, approximately 400 of the gorgeous pieces from the permanent collection are on display, and there are often special exhibits (with an extra charge). The permanent collection has good English descriptions. From the station, cross the river and go right, passing the Central Public Hall. (大阪市立東洋陶磁美術館; ☎06-6223-0055; www.moco.or.jp; 1-1-26 Naka-no-shima; adult/student/child ¥500/300/free, special exhibitions extra; ⏰9.30am-5pm, closed Mon; Ⓢ Midō-suji line to Yodoyabashi, exit 1)

O-hatsu Ten-jin

SHINTO SHRINE

3 ◉ MAP P144, C3

Hiding in plain sight amid the skyscrapers of Umeda, this 1300-year-old shrine owes its fame to one of Japan's best-known tragic plays (based on true events). Star-crossed lovers O-hatsu, a prostitute, and Tokubei, a merchant's apprentice, committed double suicide here in 1703, to remain together forever in the afterlife rather than live apart. The current shrine was constructed in 1957 (WWII destroyed the previous one); it's popular with couples, who come to pray for strength in love – and happier endings. The shrine is just southeast of Ohatsutenjin-dōri arcade. There's a flea market here the first Friday of each month. (お初天神, Tsuyu-no-Ten-jinsha; ☎06-6311-0895; www.tuyutenjin.com; 2-5-4 Sonezaki, Kita-ku; admission free; ⏰6am-midnight; Ⓢ Tanimachi line to Higashi-Umeda, exit 7, exit 15, 🚃JR Osaka, Sakurabashi exit)

National Museum of Art, Osaka

MUSEUM

4  MAP P144, A5

Originally built for Expo '70, this underground construction by architect César Pelli now houses Japan's fourth national museum. The building – like a submarine, with walls over 3m thick and light filtering down through skylights above the lobby – is interesting, and there's a decent, if not mind-blowing, collection of 20th-century works by Japanese and international artists. The entrance is marked by a large sculpture of steel tubes, said to resemble a butterfly. There's discounted admission Friday and Saturday nights (adult/student ¥250/70). (国立国際美術館; www.nmao.go.jp;

4-2-55 Naka-no-shima, Kita-ku; adult/student/child ¥430/130/free, special exhibitions extra; ⏲10am-5pm, to 8pm Fri & Sat July–mid-Oct, closed Mon; [S]Yotsubashi line to Higobashi, exit 3)

Eating

Yotaro Honten

TEMPURA ¥¥

5 MAP P144, D6

This two-Michelin-starred restaurant specialises in exceptionally light and delectable tempura served at the counter, where you can watch the chefs, or in private rooms. The tasty sea bream dish serves two to three people and the filling tempura sets are fantastic value. Look for the black-and-white sign and black slatted bars across the windows. Reserve in advance

Statue of O-hatsu and Tokubei at O-hatsu Ten-jin (p145)

through your hotel. (与太呂本店;
📞06-6231-5561; 2-3-14 Kōraibashi,
Chūō-ku; tempura sets ¥2500, sea
bream rice ¥4300; ⏰11am-1pm &
5-7pm, closed Thu; Ⓢ Sakai-suji line to
Kitahama)

Kaiten Sushi Ganko   SUSHI ¥

6 ❌ MAP P144, B3

This reliable *kaiten-sushi*
(conveyor-belt sushi) shop is a
popular choice for many a hungry
commuter, meaning the two whir-
ring tracks of plates are continu-
ously restocked with fresh options.
It can get crowded at meal times.
It's inside JR Osaka's Eki Marché
(p148) food court. (回転寿司がん
こ; 📞06-4799-6811; Eki Maré, Osaka
Station City, Kita-ku; plates ¥130-735;
⏰11am-11pm; 🚉JR Osaka, Sakurabashi exit)

Ganko Umeda Honten   JAPANESE ¥¥

7 ❌ MAP P144, B2

At the main branch of this Osaka
institution a large dining hall serves
a wide variety of set-course meals
and sushi (à la carte or in sets),
reasonably priced and made with
traditional, quality ingredients. It's
on the street along the western
side of Hankyū Umeda Station.
Look for the logo of the guy wearing a headband. (がんこ梅田本店;
📞06-6376-2001; www.gankofood.
co.jp; 1-5-11 Shibata, Kita-ku; meals
¥780-5000; ⏰11.30am-2.30am
Mon-Sat, to 11.30pm Sun; 🚉Hankyū
Umeda)

Yukari   OKONOMIYAKI ¥¥

8 ❌ MAP P144, C3

This popular restaurant in the
Ohatsutenjin-dōri arcade serves
up that great Osaka favourite,
okonomiyaki (savoury pancakes),
cooked on a griddle before you.
There's lots to choose from on the
picture menu, including vegetarian
options, but the *tokusen mikkusu
yaki* (mixed *okonomiyaki* with fried
pork, shrimp and squid) is a classic.
Look for red-and-white signage
out front. (ゆかり; 📞06-6311-0214;
www.yukarichan.co.jp; 2-14-13 Sōnezaki,
Kita-ku; okonomiyaki ¥800-1450;
⏰11am-1am; 🥢; Ⓢ Tanimachi line
to Higashi-Umeda, exit 4, 🚉JR Osaka,
south central exit)

Robatayaki Isaribi   IZAKAYA ¥¥

Head downstairs to this spirited,
friendly *izakaya* (pub eatery) near
Ganko Umeda Honten (see 7 ❌
Map p144, B2), for standards such as
skewered meats, seafood, vegies
fresh off the grill and giant pieces
of *tori no karaage* (fried chicken).
The best seats are at semicircular
counters, where your chef will
serve you using a very, very long
paddle. It's on the street along the
western side of Hankyū Umeda
Station, to the left of the signage
featuring a guy wearing a headband, and has white door curtains.
(炉ばた焼き漁火; 📞06-6373-2969;
www.rikimaru-group.com/shop/isaribi.
html; 1-5-12 Shibata, Kita-ku; dishes
¥300; ⏰5-11pm; Ⓢ Midō-suji line to
Umeda, exit 2, 🚉Hankyū Umeda)

Food Court Feasts 🍴

Eki Marché (エキマルシェ大阪; Map p144, B3; 📞06-4799-3828; www.ekimaru.com; Osaka Station City, Kita-ku; ⏰10am-10pm; 🚉JR Osaka, Sakurabashi exit) is excellent collection of wallet-friendly eateries and takeaway counters on the southwestern side of JR Osaka Station, close to Daimaru and Hotel Granvia. Top picks include Kaiten Sushi Ganko (p147), for conveyor-belt sushi, and Kani Chahan-no-Mise (p149), for delectable crab fried rice.

There are dozens of restaurants (including Japanese, French, Spanish and Chinese), plus cafes, bakeries and sweet shops on the upper floors of the Grand Front Osaka shopping mall. Most options in the **Umekita Dining food hall** (グランフロント大阪; Map p144, B2; www.gfo-sc.jp; 7th-9th fl, Grand Front Osaka South Bldg, Kita-ku; prices vary; ⏰11am-11pm; 🚉JR Osaka, north central exit, 🚉Hankyū Umeda) are midrange, with menus out front, making this a convenient place to shop around for a meal. The basement food hall **Umekita Cellar** has cheaper vendors and takeaway counters (open 10am to 10pm).

Hankyū Sanbangai   FOOD HALL ¥

9 ✕ MAP P144, B2

Beneath Hankyū Umeda Station is a long string of Japanese and international restaurants, as well as shops selling cakes, pastries and chocolates. (阪急三番街; www.h-sanbangai.com; 2nd basement fl, Hankyū Umeda Station, Kita-ku; ⏰10am-11pm; 🚉Hankyū Umeda)

Shinkiraku   TEMPURA ¥¥

This tempura specialist in the Hilton Plaza (see 10 ✕ Map p144, B3) packs 'em in at lunchtime but lacks atmosphere at dinner. The small tempura set at lunch comes with rice, miso and pickles (¥815), while the dinner set is plenty filling (¥2500). Take the escalator down to the 2nd basement floor, go right and look for the small English sign. (新喜楽; 📞06-6345-3461; 2nd basement fl, Hilton Plaza East, 1-8-16 Umeda, Kita-ku; set meals ¥980-4500; ⏰11am-3pm & 5-11pm Mon-Sat, to 10pm Sun; 🚇Yotsubashi line to Nishi-Umeda, exit 6, 🚉JR Osaka, south central exit)

Hilton Plaza   FOOD HALL ¥¥

10 ✕ MAP P144, B3

Two floors beneath the Hilton Osaka there are eight reasonably priced restaurants. Among those worth trying here is the tempura specialist, Shinkiraku. (ヒルトンプラザ; www.hiltonplaza.com; 1-8-16 Umeda, Kita-ku; ⏰11am-11pm;

Ⓢ Yotsubashi line to Nishi-Umeda, exit 6, Ⓡ JR Osaka, south central exit)

Kani Chahan-no-Mise
CHINESE ¥

This tiny shop in JR Osaka Station's Eki Marché (p148), not too far from Kaiten Sushi Ganko (see 6 ✖ Map p144, B3), serves delectable crab fried rice. There's a picture menu. (かにチャーハンの店; ☏ 06-6341-3103; Eki Maré, Osaka Station City, Kita-ku; mains from ¥780; ⏱ 10am-10.30pm; Ⓡ JR Osaka, Sakurabashi exit)

Drinking

Beer Belly
CRAFT BEER

11 🚇 MAP P144, B6

Beer Belly is run by Osaka's best microbrewery, Minoh Beer, and features Minoh's award-winning classics and seasonal offerings (pints from ¥930). Pick up a copy of Osaka's *Craft Beer Map* here to further your local beer adventures. From the subway exit, double back and take the road that curves behind the APA Hotel. (☏ 06-6441-0717; www.beerbelly.jp/tosabori; 1-1-31 Tosabori, Nishi-ku; ⏱ 5pm-2am Mon-Fri, 3-11pm Sat, 3-9pm Sun; Ⓢ Yotsubashi line to Higobashi, exit 3)

Brooklyn Roasting Company
COFFEE

12 🚇 MAP P144, D5

With its worn leather couches, big wooden communal table and industrial fittings, this is a little slice of Brooklyn in Osaka and the perfect pit stop while exploring Naka-no-shima. Sip well-crafted coffee (almond and soy milk available, too) on the wide riverside terrace and watch the boats go by. If hunger strikes, there's a small selection of doughnuts and pastries. (☏ 06-6125-5740; www.brooklynroasting.jp; 1-16 Kitahama, Chūō-ku; coffee from ¥350; ⏱ 8am-8pm Mon-Fri, 10am-7pm Sat & Sun; 🛜 Ⓢ Sakai-suji line to Kitahama, exit 2)

40 Sky Bar & Lounge
COCKTAIL BAR

13 🚇 MAP P144, B5

If heights aren't your thing, you'll need a stiff drink once you've peered down over the city from the 40th floor at this ultrasuave hotel bar. Service is impeccable and there's a good range of

---

Step Back in Time at Kissa Madura ☕

Running for 70 years, **Kissa Madura** (喫茶マヅラ; Map p144, B4; basement fl, Eki-mae Dai-1 Bldg, 1-3-1 Umeda, Kita-ku; ⏱ 8am-11pm; Ⓢ Yotsubashi line to Nishi-Umeda, exit 7a, Ⓡ JR Osaka, south central exit) is a glorious time capsule of retro-future styling, with tulip chairs, mirrors and chrome, and also vintage pricing – coffee costs just ¥250.

National Museum of Art, Osaka (p146)

ARCHITECT: CESAR PELLI, PHOTOGRAPHER: COWARDLION/SHUTTERSTOCK ©

Preparing *tako-yaki*

Street food

food and bar snacks to go with well-made cocktails. (📞06-6222-0111; www.conradhotels3.hilton.com; 3-2-4 Nakanoshima, Kita-ku, Conrad Osaka; cover after 8.30pm ¥1400; ⏰10am-midnight; Ⓢ Yotsubashi line to Higobashi, exit 2)

Salon de Amanto Tenjin

CAFE

14 Ⓣ MAP P144, D1

This cafe in a restored wooden building was the first of its kind in Nakazaki-chō – and it set off a wave of followers. Run by local performing artist Amanto Jun, it's a hub for the area's creative community. Expect tea and coffee on the menu as well as cocktails. The entrance is covered by thick foliage. (サロン・ド・アマント天人; http://amanto.jp; 1-7-26 Nakazaki-nishi, Kita-ku; ⏰noon-10pm; 📶; Ⓢ Tanimachi line to Nakazakichō, exit 4)

Moto Coffee

CAFE

15 Ⓣ MAP P144, D5

Sitting pretty in a small, white-washed building next to the Kyū-Yodogawa, Moto serves quality coffee drinks (from ¥450), along with cakes and pastries, on its riverside terrace (or upstairs if the terrace is full). (モトコーヒー; 📞06-4706-3788; www.shelf-keybridge.com/jp/moto; 2-1-1 Kitahama, Chūō-ku; ⏰noon-7pm, closed irregularly; Ⓢ Sakai-suji line to Kitahama, exit 26)

Frenz Frenzy

GAY & LESBIAN

16 Ⓣ MAP P144, D3

Frenz Frenzy calls itself a 'rainbow haven' and it means that literally: the whole place is awash in colour (including the front door, thankfully, because otherwise it would be impossible to find). Run by long-time expat Sari-chan, this is a welcoming first port of call for gay and lesbian travellers. There's no cover and drinks start at ¥500. (📞06-6311-1386; www.frenz-frenzy.website; 18-14 Kamiyama-chō, Kita-ku; ⏰8pm-1am; Ⓢ Tanimachi line to Higashi-Umeda, exit 3)

Craft Beer Base

BAR

17 Ⓣ MAP P144, A2

In the shadow of the Umeda Sky Building (p145), this bar and bottle shop specialises in local and international craft beers. Order and enjoy around the counter, or climb the narrow stairs to a small, simple white-walled room. There's a corkage fee of ¥350 to ¥500 for bottles if you drink in-house. (クラフト・ビア・ベース; www.craft-beerbase.com; 1-2-11 Ōyodo-minami, Kita-ku; draught beers ¥1000-1200; ⏰11am-11pm Fri-Wed, from 5pm Thu; Ⓢ Midō-suji line to Umeda, exit 3, Ⓡ JR Osaka, north central exit)

G Physique

GAY

18 Ⓣ MAP P144, D2

This small, long-running gay bar in Dōyama-chō is welcoming to locals and visitors alike. There's no cover charge and drinks are reasonably priced. (1st fl, Sanyo-Kaikan Bldg, 8-23 Dōyama-chō, Kita-ku; ⏰from 7pm, closing time varies; Ⓢ Tanimachi line to Higashi-Umeda, exit 3)

Windows on the World

BAR

On the 35th floor of the Hilton Osaka (see 10 ✖ Map p144, B3), this upscale yet slightly dated bar has excellent views and a good wine and whisky list. Drinks cost about ¥2000. There is a ¥1500 cover charge but this is waived during happy hour (5.30-7pm). (ウィンドーズオンザワールド; 35th fl, Hilton Osaka, 1-8-8 Umeda, Kita-ku; ⏰5.30pm-12.30am Mon-Fri, to 1am Sat & Sun; Ⓢ Yotsubashi line to Nishi-Umeda, exit 6, 🚉JR Osaka, south central exit)

Captain Kangaroo

BAR

19 🍴 MAP P144, B4

This popular, dimly lit bar in the Kita-Shinchi district is a short walk from JR Osaka Station and draws a good crowd of expats and Japanese alike. The staff speak English and are happy to pass on general Osaka tips. Among other bar-menu standard meals, they do a good burger with chunky fries. (キャプテン・カンガルー; 📞06-6346-0367; www.roo-bar.jp; 1-5-20 Sonezaki-Shinchi, Kita-ku; beer from ¥600, burgers from ¥900; ⏰6pm-5am Mon-Sat, to midnight Sun; 🚉JR Tōzai line to Kita-Shinchi, exit 3)

Entertainment

Osaka
Nōgaku Hall
THEATRE

20 ⭐ MAP P144, C2

A five-minute walk east of Hankyū Umeda Station, this theatre stages *nō* (stylised dance-drama) performances a few times each month. Look for the relief of a *nō* actor holding a fan on the facade. You'll need a Japanese speaker to call ahead about tickets. (大阪能楽会館; Osaka Nōgaku Kaikan; ☎06-6373-1726; www.nougaku.wixsite.com/nougaku; 2-3-17 Nakasaki-nishi, Kita-ku; tickets free-¥13,000; Ⓢ Tanimachi line to Nakazakichō, exit 4, ☒ Hankyū Umeda)

Shopping

Hankyū
Umeda
DEPARTMENT STORE

21 🔒 MAP P144, C3

Hankyū, which first opened in 1929, pioneered the now ubiquitous concept of the train-station department store. One of Japan's largest department stores, 'Ume-Han' is also among the most fashion-forward, with a few Japanese designers on the 3rd floor. Head to the 7th floor for artisan homewares and to the basement for a cornucopia of gourmet food items. (阪急梅田本店; www.hankyu-dept.co.jp/honten/; 8-7 Kakuda-chō, Kita-ku; ⏰10am-8pm Sun-Thu, to 9pm Fri & Sat, restaurants to 10pm; Ⓢ Midō-suji line to Umeda, exit 6, ☒ Hankyū Umeda)

Osaka Station
Shopping
🛍️

Osaka Station is ringed by malls and department stores – they're all interconnected by underground passages, making the Umeda district one big shopping conurbation. You'll find outlets of all of Japan's most popular national chains here, including Uniqlo, Muji, Tokyu Hands (p154) and Yodobashi Umeda (p155), along with literally hundreds of fashion boutiques.

Maruzen
& Junkudō Umeda
BOOKS

22 🔒 MAP P144, C1

This is the largest bookshop in Osaka, the result of two established chains joining forces. There's a big range of English-language books (on the 6th floor) and travel guides (3rd floor). It's in the Tadao Ando–designed Chaska Chayamachi building. (丸善&ジュンク堂書店梅田店; www.junkudo.co.jp; Chaska Chayamachi Bldg, 7-20 Chayamachi, Kita-ku; ⏰10am-10pm; ☒ Hankyū Umeda)

King Kong Records
MUSIC

23 🔒 MAP P144, B3

This small record store in the **Maru Building** (大阪丸ビル; www.marubiru.com/restaurant; ⏰11am-11pm) packs in a great selection of vinyl and has a friendly and knowledgable owner. (キングコング本店; ☎06-6348-2260; B1, Maru Bldg,

Local Find: Graf Studio

🛍️

Graf Studio (Map p144, A6; www.graf-d3.com; 4-1-9 Naka-no-shima, Kita-ku; ⏱11am-7pm, closed Mon; Ⓢ Yotsubashi line to Higobashi, exit 3) is a sleek furniture and design studio close to the National Museum of Art. Pick up some lovely homewares by Japanese and international designers; it stocks ceramics, jewellery and kitchenware. The attached cafe is a pleasant, quiet spot for a break.

1-9-20 Umeda, Kita-ku; ⏱11am-8pm; Ⓢ Yotsubashi line to Nishi-Umeda, exit 6, 🚆 JR Osaka, south central exit)

NU Chayamachi
DEPARTMENT STORE

24 🅐 MAP P144, C2

This series of stylish shopping centres is linked by brick paths lined with trees; it's a popular place to hang out on weekends. In addition to men's and women's fashions, look for musical instruments and a large Tower Records shop. (NU茶屋町; http://nu-chayamachi.com; 10-12 Chayamachi, Kita-ku; ⏱fashion shops 11am-9pm, Tower Records & restaurants to 11pm; 🚆 Hankyū Umeda)

Hep Five
DEPARTMENT STORE

25 🅐 MAP P144, C2

This Umeda department store has hip, youthful labels on the first six floors; fast-food restaurants, cafes and a virtual-reality game zone on the upper floors; and a bright red Ferris wheel on the roof (board from the 7th floor, ¥600). (www.hepfive.jp; 5-15 Kakuda-chō, Kita-ku; ⏱shops 11am-9pm, dining to 10.30pm, entertainment to 11pm; Ⓢ Midō-suji line to Umeda, exit 6, 🚆 Hankyū Umeda)

Hankyū Men's
DEPARTMENT STORE

26 🅐 MAP P144, C2

At 16,000 sq metres over five storeys, this is Japan's largest men's fashion retailer. Though there are a few domestic names represented here, it's mostly international brands. It's inside the Hep Navio building, adjacent to the Hankyū Umeda department store (p153). (阪急メンズ; www.hankyu-dept.co.jp/mens; Hep Navio Bldg, 7-10 Kakuda-chō, Kita-ku; ⏱11am-8pm Mon & Tue, 11am-9pm Wed-Fri, 10am-9pm Sat, 10am-8pm Sun; Ⓢ Midō-suji line to Umeda, exit 6, 🚆 Hankyū Umeda)

Tokyu Hands
DEPARTMENT STORE

Perfect for last-minute souvenir shopping is this outlet of Tokyu Hands, with the chain's signature range of must-have gadgets, homewares and stationery. Find it inside Daimaru Umeda (see 28 🅐 Map p144, B3). (東急ハンズ; www.tokyu-hands.co.jp; 10th-12th fl, Daimaru, 3-1-1 Umeda, Kita-ku; ⏱10am-9pm Mon-Sat, to 8.30pm Sun; 🚆 JR Osaka, south central exit)

Junkudō

BOOKS

27 MAP P144, B4

This large bookshop has a great selection of English-language books (on the 3rd floor) and travel guides (2nd floor). It's inside the Dōjima Avanza Building, about 10 minutes' walk from JR Osaka Station. (ジュンク堂書店; www.junkudo.co.jp; Dōjima Avanza Bldg, 1-6-20 Dōjima, Kita-ku; ☉9am-9pm; 🚃JR Tōzai line to Kita-Shinchi, exit 2)

Daimaru Umeda

DEPARTMENT STORE

28 MAP P144, B3

This huge Umeda branch of the classic Kansai department store anchors Osaka Station's southern side. On the upper floors you'll find branches of Tokyu Hands (p154), Uniqlo and the Pokemon merchandise shop, **Pokemon Centre** (ポケットモンスター; 13th fl). (大丸梅田店; 📞06-6343-1231; www.daimaru.co.jp/umedamise; South Gate Bldg, 3-1-1 Umeda, Kita-ku; ☉10am-8pm; 🚃JR Osaka, south central exit)

Yodobashi Umeda

ELECTRONICS

29 MAP P144, B2

Six floors of tech, gadgets and gizmos, plus fashion and restaurant floors. You can pick up prepaid travel SIM cards here, too. (ヨドバシ梅田; www.yodobashi-umeda.com; 1-1 Ōfuka-chō, Kita-ku; ☉shops 9.30am-10pm, restaurants 11am-11pm; Ⓢ Midō-suji line to Umeda, exit 4, 🚃JR Osaka, Midō-suji north exit)

Hankyū Umeda (p153)

Survival Guide

Tō-ji (p40) SEAN PAVONE/SHUTTERSTOCK ©

Before You Go

Book Your Stay

o Kyoto's accommodation can be booked out in the late March to early April cherry-blossom season and the November autumn-foliage season. It can also be hard to find rooms during Golden Week (29 April to 5 May) and O-bon (mid-August).

o Ryokan are traditional Japanese inns, with tatami mats on the floor and futons instead of beds. The best places serve sublime Japanese cuisine, have attentive service and beautiful rooms, often with garden views.

o Capsule hotels are simple hotels where you sleep in a small 'capsule' and use shared bathing facilities. They're fun, but be prepared for noise.

o In Osaka base yourself in Minami for access to a larger selection of bars, restaurants and shops, or in Kita for fast access to long-distance transport.

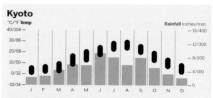

When to Go

Summer (Jun–Aug) Weather is hot and humid, but it's also the season for summer festivals.

Autumn (Sep–Nov) October and November are good times to visit, though prices and crowds increase in Kyoto during autumn-foliage season (November).

Winter (Dec–Feb) Temperatures plummet and you might see snow (making temple-hopping a chilly pursuit).

Spring (Mar–May) Weather is fantastic, and it's the cherry-blossom season (late March to early April), but accommodation is pricey and hard to find.

Useful Websites

Lonely Planet (lonely planet.com/japan/ho tels) Recommendations and bookings.

Japanese Guesthouses (www.japaneseguest houses.com) A site that specialises in ryokan bookings.

Jalan (www.jalan. net) Popular discount accommodation site, searchable in English.

Best Budget

Mosaic Machiya Hostel (www.mosaichostel. jp) Well-run hostel in an atmospheric geisha district in Kyoto.

Lower East 9 Hostel (www.lowereastnine. com) Midcentury furniture and spacious capsule dorms in Kyoto.

Hostel 64 Osaka (www.hostel64.com) Stylish hostel with a cafe/bar.

U-en (www.hostel osaka.com) Guesthouse inside an old restored town house in Osaka.

Best Midrange

Royal Park Hotel
(www.rph-the.co.jp)
The Kyoto Smart business hotel surrounded by restaurants, bars and shops.

Ryokan Uemura
(uemura.ryokan3hsl@
gmail.com) Charming ryokan in a perfect sightseeing location in Kyoto.

Kaneyoshi Ryokan
(www.kaneyosi.jp) Old favourite inn in the heart of Dōtombori, Osaka.

Arietta Hotel (www.
thehotel.co.jp) Welcoming hotel a short walk from Minami in Osaka.

Best Top End

Tawaraya (☎075-211-5566) One of the finest ryokan in Japan and located in downtown Kyoto.

Ritz-Carlton Kyoto
(www.ritzcarlton.com)
True luxury, incredible location and great views.

Four Seasons (www.
fourseasons.com/
kyoto) Luxury digs in the heart of Higashiyama, Kyoto.

Conrad Osaka (www.
conradhotels3.hilton.
com) Contemporary

glamour with incredible city views.

Swissotel Nankai Osaka (www.swissotel.
com/hotels/nankai
-osaka) Sophisticated and elegant with excellent transport options.

Arriving in Kyoto

Kansai International Airport

JR Haruka airport express The fastest and most convenient way to move between KIX and Kyoto (reserved/unreserved ¥3370/2850, 1¼ hours).

Kansai International Airport Limousine Bus
Runs frequent buses between Kyoto and KIX (about 1½ hours). Buses from Kyoto Station to the airport depart from the Hachijo-guchi exit (in front of the Avanti department store and Keihan Hotel) every 20 to 40 minutes. There are also pick-up points at Shijō Karasuma and Sanjō Keihan with departures roughly every

60 minutes. Purchase tickets from the ticket window near the boarding point.

Kyoto Station

Shinkansen (bullet trains) from Tokyo to Kyoto Station take about 2½ hours and cost around ¥13,080 for an unreserved seat. There are also *shinkansen* from cities such as Hiroshima, Osaka, Nagoya and Yokohama.

Osaka International Airport (Itami)

Osaka Airport Transport buses to Kyoto Station (¥1310, 55 minutes); shared MK taxi vans to hotels, inns and houses in Kyoto (¥2900, around one hour).

Arriving in Osaka

Kansai International Airport

Nankai Express Rapit
(¥1430, 40 minutes) All-reserved twice-hourly

service (7am to 11pm) between Nankai Kansai-Airport Station (in Terminal 1) and Nankai Namba Station; Nankai Airport Express trains take about 10 minutes longer and cost ¥920. To reach Nankai Kansai-Airport Station from Terminal 2, you will need to take a shuttle bus to Terminal 1.

JR Haruka Kansai-Airport Express Twice-hourly service (6.30am to 10pm) between KIX and Tennōji Station (unreserved seat ¥1710, 30 minutes) and Shin-Osaka Station (¥2330, 50 minutes). More frequent JR Kansai Airport rapid trains also run between KIX, Tennōji (¥1060, 50 minutes) and Osaka Station (¥1190, 68 minutes); the last train departs at 11.30pm. All these stations connect to the Midō-suji subway line. It departs from Terminal 1; you need to take a free shuttle bus if you arrive at Terminal 2.

Osaka International Airport (Itami)

Osaka Monorail Connects the airport to Hotarugaike (¥200, three minutes) and Senri-Chūō (¥330, 12 minutes), from where you can transfer, respectively, to the Hankyū Takarazaka line or Hankyū Senri line for Osaka Station.

Osaka Airport Limousine (www.okkbus.co.jp) Frequent buses connect the airport with Osaka Station (¥640, 25 minutes), Osaka City Air Terminal (OCAT; ¥640, 35 minutes) in Namba and Shin-Osaka Station (¥500, 25 minutes). At Itami, buy your tickets from the machine outside the arrivals hall.

Shin-Osaka Station

Shin-Osaka Station is on the Tōkaidō-Sanyō *shinkansen* line (between Tokyo and Hakata in Fukuoka) and the eastern terminus of the Kyūshū *shinkansen* to Kagoshima. Departures are frequent.

Destinations include Tokyo (¥14,450, 2½ hours), Hiroshima (¥10,440, 1½ hours), Hakata (¥15,000, three hours) and Kagoshima (¥21,900, 4¾ hours).

Getting Around

Subway

○ Kyoto has two efficient subway lines, operating from 5.30am to 11.30pm. Minimum adult fare is ¥210 (children ¥110).

○ The quickest way to travel between the north and south of the city is the Karasuma subway line. The line has 15 stops and runs from Takeda in the far south, via Kyoto Station, to the Kyoto International Conference Hall (Kokusaikaikan Station) in the north.

○ The east–west Tōzai subway line traverses Kyoto from Uzumasa-Tenjingawa Station in the west, meeting the Karasuma subway line at Karasuma-Oike Station, and continuing east to Sanjō-Keihan, Yamashina and Rokujizō in the east and southeast.

○ In Osaka, the JR Kanjō-sen – the Osaka loop line – makes a circuit south of JR Osaka Station, though most sights fall in the middle of it.

○ There are eight subway lines in Osaka. The one that short-term visitors will find most useful is the Midō-suji (red) line, running north–south and stopping at Shin-Osaka, Umeda (next to Osaka Station), Shinsaibashi, Namba and Tennōji stations. Single rides cost ¥180 to ¥370 (half-price for children).

○ The Metro Osaka Subway app (available from app store) is very handy to have as some subway stations in Osaka don't have a route/fare map in English. You can search for fares using the app and plan your journey.

Bus

○ Bus entry is usually through the back door and exit is via the front door.

○ Kyoto has an intricate network of bus routes providing an efficient way of getting around at moderate cost. Most of the routes used by visitors have announcements and bus stop information displays in English.

○ In Kyoto most buses run between 7am and 10pm, though a few run earlier or later.

○ In Kyoto inner-city buses charge a flat fare (¥230 for adults, ¥120 for children ages six to 12, free for those younger), which you drop into the clear plastic receptacle on top of the machine next to the driver on your way out.

○ Osaka has an extensive bus system (rides ¥210), but the train and subway network is far easier to use.

Taxi

○ Taxis are a convenient, but expensive, way of getting from place to place about town.

○ There is no need to touch the back doors of the cars at all – the opening/closing mechanism is controlled by the driver.

Kyoto Travel Passes

There's a one-day card valid for unlimited travel on Kyoto City buses and some of the Kyoto buses (these are different companies) that costs ¥600 and a one-day subway pass that also costs ¥600. A one-day unlimited bus and subway pass costs ¥900. You can buy cards from the Kyoto Tourist Information Center or any subway ticket office.

○ A taxi can usually be flagged down in most parts of both cities at any time. There are also a large number of *takushī noriba* (taxi stands), outside most train/subway stations, department stores etc.

○ In Kyoto clearly marked foreigner-friendly taxis aim to make the taxi system more accessible to tourists, with drivers who can speak other languages, such as English and Chinese, and the option to pay by credit card. There are separate taxi stands in front of the JR Kyoto Station north and south exits.

Bicycle

○ Many guesthouses hire or lend bicycles to their guests and there are also hire shops around Kyoto Station,

Osaka Travel Passes

Enjoy Eco Card (エンジョイエコカード; weekday/weekend ¥800/600, child ¥300) One-day unlimited travel on subways, city buses and Nankō Port Town line, plus some admission discounts. At subway ticket machines, push the 'English' button, insert cash, select 'one-day pass' or 'one-day pass weekend'.

Osaka Amazing Pass (大阪周遊パス; www.osp.osaka-info.jp/en/) Foreign visitors to Japan can purchase one-day passes (¥2500), good for unlimited travel on city subways, buses and trains and admission to around 35 sights (including Osaka-jō and the Umeda Sky Building); or two-day passes (¥3300) that cover the same sights but travel only on city subways and buses. Passes are sold at tourist information centres and city subway stations.

in Arashiyama and in Downtown Kyoto. With a decent bicycle and a good map, you can easily make your way all around Kyoto.

◦ Bicycle helmets are only required to be worn by law by children 12 years and under.

◦ A great place to hire a bicycle in Kyoto is the **Kyoto Cycling Tour Project** (京都サイクリングツアープロジェクト, KCTP; Map p38, D2; ☎ 075-354-3636; www.kctp.net; 552-13 Higashi-Aburanokoji-chō, Aburanokōji-dōri, Shiokōji-sagaru, Shimogyō-ku; per day from ¥1000; ⏰ 9am-6pm; 🚉 Kyoto Station).

◦ In Osaka **Hub Chari** (☎ 070-5436-2892; http://hubchari-english.

jimdo.com; per hr/day ¥200/1000) rents city bikes at several stations around town. It's run by an NGO that supports Osaka's homeless community.

Essential Information

Accessible Travel

◦ Larger train and subway stations have elevators, but they are not always obvious as these stations can be big and confusing.

◦ Station staff are helpful and courteous, even if most don't speak English.

◦ Most major sights have elevators or ramps

and usually have a few wheelchairs to loan for use inside the facilities.

◦ Larger hotels will have one or two wheelchair-friendly rooms (it's a good idea to book in advance).

◦ Pedestrianised shopping arcades, called *shōtengai*, department store restaurant halls and mall food courts are good bets for accessible dining.

◦ **Japan Accessible** (www.japan-accessible.com/index.htm) is useful for planning.

Business Hours

Banks 9am–3pm Monday to Friday

Bars 6pm–late

Department stores

10am–8pm or 9pm

Post offices local 9am–5pm Monday to Friday; central post offices 9am–7pm Monday to Friday and 9am–3pm Saturday

Restaurants 11.30am–2pm and 6pm–10pm. Last orders are usually taken 30 minutes to one hour before closing.

Shops 9am–5pm

Discount Cards

The Kansai One pass (¥3000, including ¥500 refundable deposit) is a prepaid rechargeable ICOCA transport card for foreigners offering extras such as discounts at selected tourist attractions and some temples.

Electricity

Type A
100V/60Hz

Emergency Numbers

Ambulance & Fire
☎119

Police ☎110

Internet Access

o It's getting much easier for travellers to get online in Kyoto and Osaka, with almost all accommodation offering free wi-fi and some now offering smartphones with wi-fi in hotel rooms.

o Almost all Starbucks in Japan offer free wi-fi for their customers, as do most modern cafes and some restaurants.

o If you want constant access to wi-fi when you're out and about, your best bet is either renting a portable device or buying a data-only SIM for an unlocked smartphone.

o You can buy data-only SIM cards from major electronics shops, including Yodobashi Camera and Bic Camera.

Kansai Thru Pass

The Kansai Thru Pass is a real bonus for travellers who plan to do a fair bit of exploration in the Kansai area. It enables you to ride on city subways, private railways and city buses in Kyoto, Nara, Osaka, Kōbe, Kōya-san, Shiga and Wakayama. It also entitles you to discounts at many attractions in the Kansai area. A two-day pass costs ¥4000 and a three-day pass costs ¥5200. It is available at the Kansai International Airport tourist information counter on the 1st floor of the arrivals hall and at the main bus information centre in front of Kyoto Station, among other places. For more information, visit www.surutto.com.

LGBTIQ+ Travellers

o Japan has no laws that criminalise homosexuality and open discrimination is rare; however, public display of affection (between straight couples and family members, too) is considered unusual in Japan.

o While there is a sizeable gay community in Kyoto, the gay and lesbian scene is very low-key.

o Osaka is home to Japan's second-largest gay community (after Tokyo), though it's all but invisible outside of **Dōyama-chō** (堂山町) – the neighbourhood just east of JR Osaka Station, where gay and lesbian bars are clustered.

o Osaka's pride festival, **Rainbow Festa** (www.rainbowfesta.org), takes place in October.

o **Utopia Asia** (www.utopia-asia.com/japnosak.htm) is a good resource.

Media
Magazines

o *Kansai Scene* is a free monthly publication listing art, cultural and live-music events in Kyoto and Osaka.

o The free *Kyoto Visitor's Guide* (www.kyotoguide.com) is also a good source of information on cultural and tourist events in Kyoto.

o *Kyoto Journal* (www.kyotojournal.org) is a quarterly nonprofit magazine with in-depth articles on traditional arts and culture from Japan and Asia.

Newspapers

o English-language print newspapers in Japan are the *Japan Times* and the *Japan News* (http://the-japan-news.com), which is an English version of *Yomiuri Shimbun*. *Asahi Shimbun* has an online English version (www.asahi.com/ajw).

Money

The currency in Japan is the yen (¥). The Japanese pronounce yen as 'en', with no 'y' sound. The kanji for yen is: 円.

ATMs

o ATMs are almost as common as vending machines in Japan. Un-fortunately, many do not accept foreign-issued cards.

o 7-Eleven stores and Japan Post Bank ATMs accept most international cards.

o 7-Eleven stores are the most convenient option; these are found everywhere and the ATMs are open 24 hours and have English instructions.

o You'll find Japan Post Bank ATMs in almost all post offices. These ATMs also have instructions in English.

Credit Cards

Credit cards are not as widely accepted in Japan as they are in other places, but more businesses are accepting them these days. It's always a good idea to ask in advance, though. Visa is the most widely accepted, followed by MasterCard, American Express and Diners Club.

Safe Travel

o Kyoto is generally a very safe city and crime is rare. Use common sense and follow the same precautions you normally would.

o Take care when crossing the street or exiting restaurants, hotels and shops onto the pavement; there's almost always someone on a bicycle coming your way.

o Osaka has a rough image in Japan, with the highest number of reported crimes per capita of any city in the country – though it remains significantly safer than most cities of comparable size elsewhere.

o Purse snatchings in Osaka are not uncommon so be mindful.

Smoking

Japan has a curious policy: in many cities (including Osaka and Kyoto) smoking is banned in public spaces but still allowed inside many bars and restaurants. Designated smoking areas are set up around train stations.

Toilets

o You'll come across a range of toilets when visiting Kyoto and Osaka, from futuristic gadget-laden loos to old-school squat style. When using squat toilets, the correct position is facing the hood, away from the door.

o Public toilets are free and generally clean and well-maintained. Most convenience stores have them, as do train stations and department stores. They will usually be stocked with toilet paper, but it doesn't hurt to carry small tissue packets on you just in case.

o The most common words for toilet in Japanese are トイレ (pronounced 'toire') and お手洗い ('o-te-arai'); 女 (female) and 男 (male) will also come in handy.

Money-Saving Tips

Sleep cheap You can find private rooms in business hotels, guesthouses and budget ryokan for as low as ¥5000 per person if you look around. If you're willing to share rooms in guesthouses or hostels, you can find beds for as low as ¥2500 per person.

Fine dine in the daytime Many of the finest restaurants serve pared down versions of their dinner-time fare at lunch. A *kaiseki* (Japanese haute cuisine) restaurant that can cost ¥20,000 a head at dinner might serve a lunchtime set for as little as ¥4000.

Rent a cycle Kyoto is largely flat and drivers are generally safe and courteous, making Kyoto a great city to explore on bicycle. Bike hire starts from as little as ¥500 for the day.

Buy a bus, train or subway pass Some great deals are available for Kyoto and Osaka. For details, see the boxes on p161, p162, p163.

Bentō bargain Skip dining in a restaurant all together and hit the local supermarket or the basement food floor of department stores for cheap and filling *bentō* (boxed meals).

Dos & Don'ts

Japan is well known for its etiquette, though as a visitor you are not expected to know everything. However, it does pay to familiarise yourself with a few of the main dos and don'ts.

Shoes Off You're required to remove your shoes at many temples, some museums, and most ryokan, hotels and restaurants that have tatami-mat areas. Sometimes slippers are provided. Never wear shoes or slippers on tatami mats.

Temples & Shrines There is no dress code for religious sites, but do remain respectful and speak quietly.

Queueing You'll see neat orderly queues formed when waiting for the bus, on the subway platform, at busy restaurants etc. Queue-jumping is a big no-no, so get in line.

Chopsticks Never leave them sticking upright in your bowl and never pass food from yours to another person's chopsticks; this is only done during funeral rituals.

○ Toilet slippers are provided in many bathrooms. They are only to be used in the toilet, so don't forget to take them off before you leave.

Tourist Information

Kyoto Tourist Information Center (京都総合観光案内所, TIC; Map p38, E2; ☏ 075-343-0548; 2F Kyoto Station Bldg, Shimogyō-ku; ⏰8.30am-7pm; 🚉Kyoto Station) Stocks bus and city maps, has plenty of transport info and English speakers are available to answer your questions.

Osaka Visitors Information Center Umeda (大阪市ビジターズインフォメーションセンター・梅田; Map p144; JR Osaka Station; ⏰7am-11pm; 🚉JR Osaka, north central exit) The main tourist office, with English information, pamphlets and maps, is on the 1st floor of the central north concourse of JR Osaka Station. There are also branches on the 1st floor of **Nankai Namba Station** (大阪市ビジターズインフォメーションセンター・なんば; Map p130, C5; ⏰9am-8pm; Ⓢ Midō-suji line to Namba, exit 4, 🚉Nankai Namba) and at **Kansai International Airport** (関西空港; www.kansai-airport.or.jp). Tourist offices can help book accommodation if you visit in person. The tourist information website (www.osaka-info.jp) is a good resource, too.

Visas

Visas are issued on arrival for most nationalities for stays of up to 90 days.

If asked, travellers arriving on a temporary visitor visa should be able to provide proof of onward travel or sufficient means to purchase an air or ferry ticket; in practice, this is rarely asked.

Language

Japanese pronunciation is easy for English speakers, as most of its sounds are also found in English. Note though that it's important to make the distinction between short and long vowels, as vowel length can change the meaning of a word. The long vowels (ā, ē, ī, ō, ū) should be held twice as long as the short ones. All syllables in a word are pronounced fairly evenly in Japanese. If you read our pronunciation guides as if they were English, you'll be understood.

To enhance your trip with a phrasebook, visit **lonelyplanet.com**.

Basics

Hello.
こんにちは。 *kon·ni·chi·wa*

Goodbye.
さようなら。 *sa·yō·na·ra*

Yes.
はい。 *hai*

No.
いいえ。 *ī·e*

Please.
ください。 *ku·da·sai*

Thank you.
ありがとう。 *a·ri·ga·tō*

Excuse me.
すみません。 *su·mi·ma·sen*

Sorry.
ごめんなさい。 *go·men·na·sai*

How are you?
お元気ですか? *o·gen·ki des ka*

Fine. And you?
はい、元気です。 *hai, gen·ki des*
あなたは? *a·na·ta wa*

Do you speak English?
英語が *ē·go ga*
話せますか? *ha·na·se·mas*
ka

I don't understand.
わかりません。 *wa·ka·ri·ma·sen*

Eating & Drinking

I'd like to reserve a table for (two).
(2人)の *(fu·ta·ri) no*
予約をお *yo·ya·ku o*
願いします。 *o·ne·gai shi·mas*

I'd like (the menu).
(メニュー) *(me·nyū)*
をお願いします。 *o o·ne·gai shi·mas*

I don't eat (red meat).
(赤身の肉) *(a·ka·mi no ni·ku)*
は食べません。 *wa ta·be·ma·sen*

That was delicious.
おいしかった。 *oy·shi·kat·ta*

Please bring the bill.
お勘定 *o·kan·jō*
をください。 *o ku·da·sai*

Cheers! 乾杯! *kam·pai*

beer ビール *bī·ru*

coffee コーヒー *kō·hī*

Shopping

I'd like ...
…をください。 *... o ku·da·sai*

I'm just looking.
見ているだけです。 *mi·te i·ru da·ke des*

How much is it?
いくらですか？ *i·ku·ra des ka*

That's too expensive.
高すぎます。 *ta·ka·su·gi·mas*

Can you give me a discount?
ディスカウント *dis·kown·to*
できますか？ *de·ki·mas ka*

Emergencies

Help!
たすけて！ *tas·ke·te*

Go away!
離れろ！ *ha·na·re·ro*

Call the police!
警察を呼んで！ *kē·sa·tsu o yon·de*

Call a doctor!
医者を呼んで！ *i·sha o yon·de*

I'm lost.
迷いました。 *ma·yoy·mash·ta*

I'm ill.
私は病 *wa·ta·shi wa*
気です。 *byō·ki des*

Where are the toilets?
トイレは *toy·re wa*
どこですか？ *do·ko des ka*

Time & Numbers

What time is it?
何時ですか？ *nan·ji des ka*

It's (10) o'clock.
(10)時です。 *(jū)·ji des*

Half past (10).
(10)時半です。 *(jū)·ji han des*

morning	朝	*a·sa*
afternoon	午後	*go·go*
evening	夕方	*yū·ga·ta*
yesterday	きのう	*ki·nō*
today	今日	*kyō*
tomorrow	明日	*a·shi·ta*
1	一	*i·chi*
2	二	*ni*
3	三	*san*
4	四	*shi/yon*
5	五	*go*
6	六	*ro·ku*
7	七	*shi·chi/na·na*
8	八	*ha·chi*
9	九	*ku/kyū*
10	十	*jū*

Transport & Directions

Where's the ...?
…はどこ *... wa do·ko*
ですか？ *des ka*

What's the address?
住所は何 *jū·sho wa nan*
ですか？ *des ka*

Can you show me (on the map)?
(地図で)教えて *(chi·zu de) o·shi·e·te*
くれませんか？ *ku·re·ma·sen ka*

When's the next (bus)?
次の(バス)は *tsu·gi no (bas) wa*
何時ですか？ *nan·ji des ka*

Does it stop at ...?
…に *... ni*
停まりますか？ *to·ma·ri·mas ka*

Please tell me when we get to ...
… に着いたら *... ni tsu·i·ta·ra*
教えてください。 *o·shi·e·te ku·da·sai*

Index

See also separate subindexes for:

❸ **Eating** p171

◉ **Drinking** p172

✪ **Entertainment** p172

🔒 **Shopping** p172

Sights 000
Map Pages **000**

Behind the Scenes

Send Us Your Feedback

We love to hear from travellers – your comments help make our books better. We read every word, and we guarantee that your feedback goes straight to the authors. Visit **lonelyplanet.com/contact** to submit your updates and suggestions.

Note: We may edit, reproduce and incorporate your comments in Lonely Planet products such as guidebooks, websites and digital products, so let us know if you don't want your comments reproduced or your name acknowledged. For a copy of our privacy policy visit lonelyplanet.com/privacy.

Kate's Thanks

Thank you again to Laura Crawford for the opportunity to work on Osaka and Kyoto, and to Jen Carey for your help throughout. Huge thanks to Kengo Nakao from the Kyoto Tourist Information office for your assistance. Thanks to my parents for joining me in Kyoto, and keeping up the research pace in the extreme heat! And to my friend Yuki and my fiancé Trent for great nights out, loads of food and rock bar shenanigans. Thanks also to all the in-house staff at Lonely Planet who make this book happen.

Acknowledgements

Cover photograph: Kiyomizu-dera, Kyoto, Benny Marty/Alamy ©

This 2nd edition of Lonely Planet's *Pocket Kyoto & Osaka* guidebook was researched and written by Kate Morgan. The previous edition was researched and written by Kate Morgan and Rebecca Milner. This guidebook was produced by the following:

Destination Editors Laura Crawford, James Smart

Senior Product Editor
Kate Chapman

Product Editor
Rachel Rawling

Regional Senior Cartographer
Diana Von Holdt

Assisting Cartographer
Michael Garrett

Book Designer
Jessica Rose

Assisting Editors
Naoko Akamatsu, Judith Bamber, Imogen Bannister, Katie Connolly, Kate James

Cover Researcher
Brendan Dempsey-Spencer

Thanks to
William Koh, Kathryn Rowan

Our Writers

Kate Morgan

Having worked for Lonely Planet for over a decade now, Kate has been fortunate enough to cover plenty of ground working as a travel writer on destinations such as Shanghai, Japan, India, Russia, Zimbabwe, the Philippines and Phuket. She has done stints living in London, Paris and Osaka, but these days is based in one of her favourite regions in the world: Victoria, Australia. In between travelling the world and writing about it, Kate enjoys spending time at home working as a freelance editor.

Published by Lonely Planet Global Limited
CRN 554153
2nd edition – Aug 2019
ISBN 978 1 78657 852 5
© Lonely Planet 2019 Photographs © as indicated 2019
10 9 8 7 6 5 4 3 2 1
Printed in Malaysia